The books to come

Foreword by Jenni Quilter

Alan Loney

Grateful acknowledgment is given to Peter Koch and The Codex Foundation for permission to reprint *Each new book*, which first appeared in the CODE(X)+1 monograph series (2009) and to Kyle Schlesinger at Cuneiform Press for reprinting *Meditatio: the printer printed: manifesto* (2004). "What book does my library make" was presented in the Threads Talk Series (2009) and is available online at PennSound. An earlier version of "The limits of the book as object" was presented at the BSANZ conference in Brisbane, Australia (2009). *Zephyros : the book untitled* was printed by the author as a limited edition at Electio Editions, Melbourne (2007).

The author expresses special gratitude to Francis McWhannell and Jed Birmingham for their sharp, insightful editing and proofing of the text.

Distributed by:
Small Press Distribution
1341 Seventh Street
Berkeley, CA 94710-1403
510-524-1668 or toll-free
800-869-7553
www.spdbooks.org

Address all inquiries to:
Cuneiform Press
University of Houston-Victoria
School of Arts and Sciences
3007 North Ben Wilson
Victoria, TX 77901
www.cuneiformpress.com

∞ The paper on which this book is printed meets the minimum requirements of American National Standard for Information Sciences — Permanence of Paper for Printed Library Materials, ANSI z39.48–1984.

LCCN: 2010935025
ISBN: 978-0-9860040-1-8

This book was made possible, in part, through the generous support of the School of Arts and Sciences, University of Houston-Victoria and friends of Cuneiform Press.

The books to come

CUNEIFORM PRESS / 2012

ACKNOWLEDGMENTS

Some of these essays have previously appeared in other contexts and I wish to express my sincere gratitude to the following : Peter Koch and The Codex Foundation for permission to reprint *Each new book*, which first appeared in the CODE(X)+1 monograph series 2009; Kyle Schlesinger at Cuneiform Press for *Meditatio : the printer printed : manifesto* 2004; Steve Clay and Kyle Schlesinger for 'What book does my library make', delivered as a talk in Granary's Threads Talk Series 2009. 'The limits of the book as object' was given in an earlier version as a paper at the BSANZ conference in Brisbane, Australia 2009. *Zephyros : the book untitled* was printed as a limited edition at Electio Editions, Melbourne 2007. Thanks are due also to Jed Birmingham for his sharp-eyed reading of the initial text, and to Francis McWhannell I extend my deepest appreciation for his patient and skillful editing. For this book, my heartfelt thanks go to Kyle Schlesinger for his belief in the project and to Jenni Quilter for her insightful Foreword.

Aside from the immediate process of these essays there is a longer history of engagement with others, without whose encouragement and conversation much in these pages could not have happened. Some are sadly no longer with us and all I can do here is merely hint at the privilege and honor I have known : Bill Wieben, J E Traue, Roderick Cave, Denis Glover, Janet Paul, Edgar Mansfield, Arthur Johnson, Lewis Allen, Robert Creeley, Max Gimblett, Peter Simpson, Caroline Williams, Penny Griffith, Elizabeth Wilson, Crispin Elsted, Steve Clay, Peter Crisp, Chris Wallace-Crabbe, Peter H Hughes, Marion May Campbell, Bruno Leti. To my partner Miriam Morris I owe more than I can say for her unfailing support and belief in my printing/poetic life, and it gives me the greatest pleasure to dedicate this book to her.

— Alan Loney
2010

CONTENTS

FOREWORD

You have this book in your hands. You've opened the cover,
turned the endpapers, glanced briefly at the title page, and
now your eye settles — like a moth, like someone sighting
land — onto this page.

This is not where Alan Loney himself would begin. "Even
now," he writes, "I rarely read a book from cover to cover."
Instead, he reads in fragments and out of sequence, troubled by the assumption that to begin with the foreword and
read from beginning to end is the most comprehensive way to
understanding a writer's meaning. He is not interested in the
authority this kind of reading brings.

He also discourages the reader who would hope to find in
these pages a tidy account of his life as a poet and publisher.
Loney (b. 1940) is the author of more than thirteen books of
poetry and prose. He has founded three presses (Hawk Press,
Black Light Press and most recently, Electio Editions) and has
directed publications at The Holloway Press at The University
of Auckland. In total, he has designed, typeset (by hand),
printed and bound more than fifty books. From 1971 onwards,

he has devoted his life to words and books, but in this book he resists the kind of *ethos* that these biographical facts bring to his thinking on, in his words, "the life, death, and erotics of the body of the book". *The books to come* is a tangled forest — in New Zealand terms, a tough piece of bush — designed to resist our patient endeavors. Its effect is fragmentary, almost Heraclitean in parts, and we move from paragraph to paragraph, from sun to shadow and back again, adjusting, refocusing, staring, and slowly coming to understand in broader, almost convulsive ways. *Ah, we think. He sees what we stopped seeing a long time ago. He is asking us to look at what was in front of us all along.*

You have this book in your hands. Try noticing it. Try experiencing it as an object. Turn the pages, and pick a landing in amongst his words. Try skipping out. Try coming back.

"My main interest in books," Loney writes, "had been in what most people regard as the least significant aspects, that is, everything aside from reading." And later: "the two piles of hand-cut handmade paper on my bench this morning are beautiful to me — very beautiful, as if I had suddenly understood after all this time that it is paper that makes a book, and more so than type or words or images." We easily overlook the feel of the paper and the way the words look on the page. We might fetishize the book as object (first-editions, sentimental copies) but this gaze is directed towards a book rather than the book as principle and process in conveying information. For instance, most readers have no idea of the history behind the book's design conventions or why they continue to replicate these principles electronically. "You don't have to know anything about typographical history," Loney writes, "just how to use the [computer] software. You don't have to know anything about how the options came to be the options..." He argues that we tend to use the words "text" and "book" and "printed matter" interchangeably, when only one of these words exclusively describes a sequence of pages collected together in codex form. If we use one term in place of another, we risk misunderstanding and eventually devaluing (or ignoring) the worth of a book's form because we are only interested in what a text says rather than what it does on the page. It's a suitably thorny irony that this foreword is really a response to Loney's text and not his book. That physical eventuality is yet to come; I don't know the cover's color, the type or paper Cuneiform Press will use. The characters on my screen are very different to how they appear now, in front of you. And even as a reader, your focus on the sense that these characters make in your mind will tend to make the book disappear, or at least, move into the background of your consciousness.

The book is a vulnerable object in these pages, jerked this way and that by technology, liable to pulping by book publishers and the epistemological elisions of academics. Loney feels the mortality of books keenly and he is worried about the survival of his own, but he is relentless in the interrogation of this anxiety as well. Indeed, this interrogation is a central feature in this collection of essays; even as Loney eulogizes the unread and remaindered, encouraging us with a kind of negative capability to champion the book by its near misses and misidentifications, he is also quick to recognize the book's limits, the inevitability of its destruction, to remind himself of the precedence of oral cultures and his own bardic allegiances as a poet. Loney can see the reason of the world, its secular and rational eventualities, but that still does not help him; he is afraid for his books, for others' books, for the books to come, and his writing pours from the knowledge that this could be resolved, but isn't — stubbornly, insistently isn't. It is a feature of these essays that they remain resolutely unsettled. Even their style is protean; the text shifts from poetry to prose, fragment to episode. If Loney could preside over a world in which the book was king, where every word was recorded and read and kept alive, where the word "book" only referred to the distinct form of a book (as he puts it, "codex + text") and nothing else, I'm sure that Loney would remain troubled, writing "it is still hard for me to accept that the book's form might have to be accepted as an unquestionable given. And as hard for me to depart from it." Even as he champions the book, he ends up holding it at arm's length, and as Loney has pointed elsewhere in The Falling, to keep one's distance through language is to embrace the ambivalence of the verb "to keep"; to suffer distance and never let it go, no matter how far away you are.

Loney's own books are barely mentioned here; they exist as a world of shadows. Further, we do not know why (in his words), "He is one of the most regularly reviled poets in the country of his birth over some twenty-five years." We are left to surmise the reasons as to why he moved from New Zealand to Melbourne, Australia, where he now lives. Loney's biography is suppressed here in order to establish a plangent authority that derives from imagining the book as principle in a series of perspectival propositions: "how may I understand this — over all the planet millions of words in unrelated & related languages are at this moment not being read, and many won't be. What can be uttered about these words. Can 'words' even be a proper term for them." These conceptions jerk us up out of the particular — and for a moment, we have an out-of-book experience, consider what's between our hands with both detachment and vigor, seeing it as a marvelous object whose proportions are newly odd. Loney asks, "by what lore is the book bound", and we pause at these questions that are not questions, these flattened requests, and start to understand that the lore by which this text is bound is his restless eye and mind, his grief and puzzlement over the meaning of the book. *The books to come* is remarkable in its persistent vulnerability. It courts our uncertainty and our patience, provoking us into reconsidering our relationship to the book and, I imagine, to this book, the paper in your hands. Watch how these words slope down, slowly pouring their way towards the centre crease of the page.

Eventually you'll close this book, and place it on your shelf. There it will sit alongside others and (to echo Loney's own description), your eye will acquaint itself with the shape of its spine. You'll look at it idly, often when you are thinking about something else. The pages' vegetal matter is pulped and pressed, and the ink remains, letter touching letter, the universe collapsed as neatly as an accordion, ready to expand again. Reading these essays, I have found myself imagining the forest from which this book will come, the quiet trees and the feel of the air between them. I usually do not think of this kind of sacrifice that goes into making a book, but Loney puts me there, looking out of my window in New York City, longing for the knowledge that will stretch out in a ghostly wake behind this text when it becomes a book. The issue of physical form haunts him, and it haunts me now too.

And hopefully, remarkably, the book will be opened up by you again, then put away. And again. And again.

— Jenni Quilter
New York University

Meditatio : the printer printed : manifesto

Among the messages the computer has for us, in an awful
conjunction of opportunity and betrayal, is that poetry and
typography exist in an alliance as creative as it is deadly. The
computer allows us to compose directly into print. In doing
so it bypasses handwriting. It allows us to cleanly alter what
we key in. In doing so it erases the archive of our composition-
al gestures. The custom of taking handwriting and printing
as historically successive allows us to study the differences
between them. In doing so we obscure the reality that handwriting and printing exist in complex, current, simultaneous
dynamics. Accepting that poetry and typography are in intimate relation with each other, we should not forget that while
all poetry is typographic, not all typography is poetry. Poetry
and typography exist in 'twin histories', histories not necessarily co-terminus with each other, yet bound in an equation
that can be stated : Where there is poetry, there is typography.
In this essay I will meditate on various aspects of this equation and take a stand or set of stands, as manifesto, on my
own practice as poet and printer.

¶ As a poet I should say I am no theorist. I have as it happens no academic training at all, but my every writing/reading day is dependent upon the labour of scholars and the mostly scholarly presses and journals that publish them. I have also found some of the smaller works of major theorists very useful in my own thinking. I can cite the work of Foucault in *This is not a pipe* and regard the essays by Blanchot and Foucault on each other as a beautiful kind of acknowledgment. If there is a work written by another that I would like to have written, it is Jacques Derrida's 'Envois' in *The Post Card*. There is continuing interest for me in Heidegger, Wittgenstein, A N Whitehead, Jane Ellen Harrison and the radial writing and other notions of Jerome McGann, Randall McLeod, and D F McKenzie. If I were to say whose essays I admired I'd say Hugh Kenner's *The Pound Era* and Guy Davenport's *The Geography of the Imagination*. And Robert Creeley, Charles Olson, Ezra Pound, Gertrude Stein, Hilda Doolittle, Susan Howe and Anne Carson writing on anything. In the wider tradition there is Sappho, the pre-Socratics, Homer, Catullus, Ovid, Chaucer, Shakespeare, Keats, Dickinson, Donne. I want to read deeply rather than widely. The wide and various reading done by both writing and non-writing friends is beyond me. If there is a single sign that tells me of my deep inadequacy as a reader in the context in which I am at this moment writing, it is not the theses and arguments of others, it is their footnotes.

¶ As a printer I am involved in another history. I have written elsewhere that in New Zealand the emergent poetry canon

and the book production values in which it was published
were in the hands of the same people. The poetry behind
that small revolution in the 1930s was aligned with Pound &
Eliot (not Pound & Stein) and W H Auden, Stephen Spender,
Cecil Day Lewis and Louis MacNeice. The associated book
production values were aligned with those of their publishers, Oxford University Press, Hogarth Press, Jonathan Cape,
Faber & Faber, Random House and Victor Gollanz. Behind
that alignment in turn were the writings of Stanley Morison,
Bruce Rogers, Beatrice Warde, D B Updike, Eric Gill, Frederic
Goudy, and the publications of such as The Nonesuch Press
and The Monotype Corporation. This period, 1920s to 1940s,
was one in which scholarly activity influenced commercial book production in visible and articulate ways. When I
began printing in 1974, the models immediately and locally
available were the university-based presses of D F McKenzie
(Wai-te-ata Press, Victoria University of Wellington), Keith
Maslen (The Bibliography Room, University of Otago), print-
er/poet Denis Glover at his Caxton Press (Christchurch),
and the fine printing collections at the Alexander Turnbull
Library in Wellington. Within two years I was reading
Roderick Cave's *The Private Press*, Clifford Burke's *Printing
Poetry*, Lewis Allen's *Printing with the Handpress* and Sandra
Kirshenbaum's *Fine Print* magazine — a nice mix of what
was possible in the field, how to go about it, and how it was
talked about. Between 1974 and 1979, my practice changed
from making the books I published to publishing the books
I made, and this shift from publisher to printer is crucial for
all else I have done in the field.

¶ What was a great, and greatly resisted, turn in typographical practice early in the twentieth century, was the introduction of asymmetric typography. Dada, Surrealism, Constructivism, Futurism all contributed to an altered view of what sort of thing a page was, and how anyone might conduct themselves upon it. These movements knew how they were reacting to the mainstreams of their day, and those mainstreams were very clear about proper typographical behaviour. I can only simplify here, but new ideas of the page or two-page spread as a field in which anything can happen anywhere on the paper threatened (and it was threatening to those who resisted it) the then current disposition of type within the rectangular letterpress type block and its placement on a central axis within the block. The change received detailed articulation in the writings of Jan Tschichold whose work was controversial but very influential. The conflict between symmetric and asymmetric typographic arrangement is long over. Both have now been incorporated into more or less neutral options available to designers and printers, even to the point of using both within the one book. I have often been intrigued to see radically shaped poetry published in which the whole of the inside of the book is asymmetrical but the cover and/or titlepage text is centered on the page. When there is nothing in the content of the work to make such a decision an exemplification then it looks like merely surfing the options. My own view is more one-eyed. While I have occasionally broken my rule, my rule is asymmetry every time, every page, every book — even where my writing is printed or published by others. It is just part of the deal when I offer my texts for publication.

For those for whom centered typography was historically important, production values contained the design values of the day. But if I can distinguish production values from design values, then I can accept traditional standards of typographical arrangement, impression and binding without accepting centered layouts. If my poems are asymmetrically arranged, with titles set-left, then I want every other page in the book to follow thru with that fact. If one is going to design a book so all its parts are in an overt relation with one another, then the shape of the text is the primary design datum upon which all other decisions are to be made. Loading an asymmetric poem with a symmetric titlepage or cover does violence to the just shaping of the poem.

¶ Centered pages, with poem titles and page numbers centered, have their origins in the development of printerly conventions. The centering is not done in relation to the way the poem looks on the page. If a book has some poems with short lines and some with long lines (i.e. the usual case) then centering has to have a basis to work on (i.e. centered on what?) and the standard situation was to center the titles and folios 'on the measure'. The measure is the length of the line within the rectangle of type-metal that makes up the letterpress block. The measure is not the optical width of the poem. It means that the spatial relationships between the centered material and the set-left material of the poem will differ from poem to poem. Centering is a printer's convention because it makes the printer's life easier when composing the types. 'Center everything' means you don't have to make separate and time-consuming (=money-consuming) aesthetic decisions about the title and folios for every book. The same goes for titlepages, cover texts, contents pages, and the copyright page which also carries the publisher's details and library cataloging data. If one's poetry/poetic questions conventional modalities of cultural behaviour, then the books to be issued might also have conventional modalities that are worth making separate decisions about. The problem with the computer and its capacity for typesetting is that it erases the histories of the practices upon which its array of click-on options is based. You don't have to know anything about typographical history, just how to use the software. You don't have to know anything about how the options came to be the options, just how to click on the options you 'want'. The computer includes and elides the whole historical and often bitter debate between symmetric and asymmetric typography. It has no idea, for example, that English printing scholar Stanley Morison eventually took the view that books should always be symmetric, and that asymmetry should be confined to advertising as a lesser mode of typographical and cultural being. For Morison, in other words, the question 'whether symmetry or asymmetry' was bound up with beliefs about the hierarchical and cultural value of social practices.

¶ The relation 'symmetry/asymmetry' is not itself symmetrical when it comes to typographical practice. In symmetrical arrangements the major choices available to the typographer are vertical, that is, in how much space there is to be between lines &/or where on the page, up or down, the lines are to be placed. In asymmetrical arrangements the page becomes a field in which both vertical and horizontal choices are of more or less equal value. In symmetry the choices are fixed without recourse to the text. In asymmetry the choices can be made in relation to the text, even if that sets up what turns out to be conventional for that book, e.g. the folios appear in one position on all rectos and in another on all versos. The one is conventional for all books, the other conventional for that book only. There is still enough in the current usages of both for me to feel that the issue is still alive for our practice even if the discussion about them seems to have long since passed.

¶ The early illuminated manuscript herbal is a great place to see the page or double spread as a field in which any mark can be situated in any position. Hand-drawn or painted plants branching all over the page can have texts hand-written between the stems, flowers and roots, text and image weaving in and out of each other in something like a unified field. When herbals came to be printed, however, two main things happened. First, the illustrations were immediately less florid, often monochrome, and limited in complexity and position by what the new technologies of printing and engraving could accommodate in the locked-up forme. Second, the text was now confined to the rectangular block of type required by these technologies, and only rarely was the printing press used to emulate the possibilities of manuscript. Since the advent of printing the relations between text and image have been determined by the rectangular frame, a frame inside the frame of the page itself. I have often thought that the computer might have permitted a return to the interweave of text and image, the kind visible in the manuscript herbal. But just as printing was developed to imitate the manuscript book of the day, a book primarily of text with illuminations after the event, so the computer has imitated the letterpress printed book without having the rectangular forme as a technical necessity. We are thus still designing books on computers as if they were to be printed by letterpress. A letterpress Penguin book of the 1920s looks much like an offset Penguin of the present, even tho the technologies that produced both are radically different.

¶ When it comes to fine press books, letterpress remains the primary means of production, and hand-set or machine-set metal type is the means by which the text is impressed upon the page. Type sizes are limited in contrast to the size range in computers, and the range of types is limited now that most of the major metal type suppliers all over the world have gone out of business in response to computer typesetting and offset printing. For some fine printers however these limitations are no longer fully determinative, and the recently developed photopolymer plate has allowed them to combine computer typesetting with letterpress machining. Types that are no longer available in metal can be found on computer, as are types that were never in metal at all. So, if the computer can give us the page as a unified field, as in the manuscript herbals, then those fields can be printed letterpress using photopolymer plates.

¶ On the other hand, the early twentieth century has given us a number of examples of, just let me call them 'field objects', which are printed letterpress. Works by Iliazd (Ilia Zdanevitch), H N Werkman, M Levé (printer of Apollinaire's *Il Pleut*), Ardengo Soffici, El Lissitzky and others are *tours de force* in letterpress terms as they break up the visual rectangle of the letterpress forme — even tho that forme would have been used to hold the typographical elements together. If one had to make a case for the computer and layout by field, the fact that such layouts were achieved brilliantly in letterpress would render the task a lot easier.

¶ I am about to start printing again after a break of just over five years. The question is: How am I to make fine books in a world of diminishing letterpress resources and changing technologies? In the past I used photopolymer plates for visual images, never for text. I like type. I like building up the words letter by letter, varying the mechanical word-spacing to deal with the optical difference, for example, of adjacent words ending and beginning with lower case 'l', from adjacent words ending and beginning with lower case 'w'. Or, in setting 14pt Monotype Centaur, sliding a copper half-point space between lower case 'u' and 'r' in words like 'our', 'your' etc, because the set widths do not work with these two letters in this size and they simply appear too close together. These tiny adjustments are part of what the craft of printing is all about for me and I foresee little or no use of photopolymers for text in the work ahead. H N Werkman used what was already in the print-shop for his prints and for the works in his periodical *The next call*.

All letterpress print-shops had limited means. I think few who have grown up with computers have any idea how limited were the type holdings of letterpress printers, in spite of the array of types on offer from the major type suppliers. The sheer and somewhat adamantine givens of a small print-shop are far more interesting to me than the vast array of computer typefaces and the symbols that accompany them. In the same way that the twenty-six letter alphabet is a finite range with indefinite possibility, the few givens of the print-shop are capable of an indefinite number of arrangements in proximity, position, color on various textures, sizes and colors of paper. At present I am having to furnish a printery from the beginning, so my range of givens is even smaller than it was after twenty-five years of collecting items as they became available. I am used, however, to designing on the stone or on the press itself with these elements. Instead of drawing patterns and looking for things in the printery that will reproduce them, I have often used the physical elements themselves, moving them about on the press until I have a result which fits my sense of the work at hand. While I have designed with type, I have never, as Johanna Drucker has, composed in type, never created the text on the press with bits of lead and wood rather than with bits of hand-writing or computer setting.

¶ Fine press books do not generally get very good press from art theorists and practitioners. Unless one's work can be re-identified as an 'artist's book', there can be a quick relegation of one's work to mere 'craft', or worse, to the mere making of a pretty book which could just as well have been a nice trade edition. There are times when I think that it is only the quality of the artist that differentiates one book from another when all other aspects of the book's manufacture are of the same order. If a good text is printed by hand with lithographs by an artist such as Robert Motherwell, it will often be acceptable 'as art' while the same text printed in the same way by the same press but with lithographs by an artist with little skill and no reputation is not. The problem can slide across, as it were, from being one of degree to being one of kind. But in my view these are matters of degree. Support for this view comes from an interesting place — recent scholarly work on the history of the artist's book. Studies by Riva Castleman, Johanna Drucker, and others all complicate the notion of the artist's book, and partly in an attempt to posit a history for the apparent genre. For Castleman for instance the notion of the artist's book stretches back to the livre d'artiste of the late nineteenth century which was produced by a publisher who brought author and artist together in a book designed and produced by the publisher. The texts might be cut in wood or engraved in metal or set in letterpress, but it was the publisher (Eduard Pelletan, Ambroise Vollard, Henry Kahnweiler, Albert Skira, Tériade) who ran the show, put up the money, and directed the artist, sometimes page by page, sometimes giving the artist enough licence to influence the whole process. There is no way of side-stepping these works as publications in which the artist had a limited role. Later book artist Iliazd was his own publisher, designer and letterpress printer who brought artists into the work by giving them specific texts to which to respond, but very much under his direction. The work of

Iliazd, it seems to me, cannot escape description as the work of a fine press, and the fact that his artists included Picasso, Miró, Matisse, Giacometti, Villon and Ernst cannot gainsay this point. Of course we are now in the position to propose that some works are definable in a number of ways and that 'artist's book' and 'fine press book' may equally, and without violence to the other, apply.

¶ Australian artist Bruno Leti is a painter, printmaker and maker of artist's books. His books are artist's books in a very literal sense. He chooses a text, makes images in response to or in conversation with it, prints the images either by print-making processes or even by laser print (on his own machine), may have the text printed by screen-printing or laser print, and designs the binding which is given to another to execute. Here, all aspects of the book are under the artist's direction and control. The work is 'his' book — specifically, the artist has made the book &/or has others perform part of its making to his specification. This is very different from the *livre d'artiste*, and equally different from the works of Iliazd. These distinctions ought to be preserved in the ways we talk about books, but in the prevailing modes of such talk the distinctions are blurred or perhaps simply gathered together in order to maintain the notion of 'artist's book' as a genre with a history long enough and broad enough to validate our own activity on the one hand and our scholarly endeavour on the other. I have in principle no argument with this procedure, but if one is going to adopt it *and* have a negative exclusion-ary approach to press books at the same time, then one falls into the trap of failing to acknowledge the crossover points where the books of Iliazd for example can be understood as belonging in both categories — artist's book, fine press book — with equal validity. But the artist's book, as an object made by, or under the explicit direction of, the artist, is a category worth maintaining, particularly as this is the one modality in which the term 'artist's book' has this literal force : *an artist's book is a book made by an artist*. If one looked at the works of Iliazd as artist's books, are they Iliazd's artist's books or are they the artist's books of Matisse, Picasso, Giacometti, and so on. For me the question always is : Who is the artist, and how much of a role did the artist have in the project. This is at least a way into the vexed problems surrounding the identification and definition of just what sort of thing do we have in hand in any instance. There is, however, an interesting parallel in the definition by Joseph Moxon in his *Mechanical Exercises on the Whole Art of Printing* (1683-84) of 'typographer': 'By a typographer I mean such a one who can either perform, or direct others to perform, all the Handyworks and Physical Operations relating to Typography'. H N Werkman performed his own typography, Jan Tschichold directed others. Replace Moxon's 'typographer' with 'artist's book maker' and his 'typography' with 'artist's books', and you have a clear sense of what I am suggesting.

¶ William Blake stands here as an intriguing example. Most of his works are known to us primarily as works of literature. They are published as literature, as if the colorful hand-engraved books which allow anybody to know they exist at all are merely acts of decoration, even a writing out by hand and 'coloring in' — Blake's own treatment being merely one among an indefinite number of potential other 'treatments'. The literary prejudice that Johanna Drucker describes in *The Visible Word* against the coloring or shaping of words is embedded in the very way in which these works are published in carefully 'accurate' editions. Happily, in Blake's case, this notion has been under close scrutiny for some time in the spheres of bibliography and textual studies, particularly in the writings of Jerome McGann. The upshot of these attentions is that Blake's works are under-read if the words are isolated from their otherwise richly signifying contexts. So how is the term 'artist's book' to be employed if we are not to obscure important distinctions between different modalities of making. The problem of naming is still an issue when it comes to how non-practitioners and non-specialists refer to the often unusual-looking objects they can find in their company. In my experience many people are remarkably resistant to rethinking what they have always assumed they know and do not have to re-learn about the book.

¶ I do not make artist's books. I make fine press books. But I recognise vividly, and on a personal level, this problem : the artist's and art theorist's rejection of my work because art is not supposed to be literary, in spite of the widespread use of words in paintings, and the poet's and literary theorist's rejection of the work because it seems one is merely loading fancy typography and materials onto a poetry which ought somehow to be able to 'stand on its own'. As Johanna Drucker found that her art seemed to get lost in the gap between these two responses, so press books also get lost there, altho for different reasons. Even when I have made books in which the visual matter is not a reproduction of anything that exists outside the book, when the book itself is the original art, I was not able to dent these twin prejudices that my work encountered in New Zealand. By contrast, in Australia there seems nothing I can do to prevent my books being described by almost everyone who sees them (except some librarians) as artist's books. There are clearly no handy definitions that can stick or can be adequately conveyed or can counter the language used by others in their scholarly or artistic projects.

¶ What happens when the printer is to be printed by a private or fine press, and one which is used to exercising its own particular tyranny in the print-shop? For my own artistic project is not merely that I write sometimes and sometimes I print, altho that is true. And while I seek trade publication for some of my texts, I also want to see my books receive print by fine printers who are thoughtful and skilful in their work in ways that I recognise and admire. It was not until I retired from printing in late 1998 that I began to have this particular urge and I have since been honoured to have a small number of my texts so received by other presses. There is a rough and ready definition of a private press, which states that private printers are those who print what they like, how they like, when they like. According to this, the private press printer is in full charge of what happens in the printery, in terms both of overall policy and of the minutest detail of typographic and printerly practice. For twenty-five years I took almost no notice at all of what authors wanted or artists preferred. As far as I was concerned, so long as my settings followed the text with absolute fidelity to its spacing as defined by the author, and so long as the artist acknowledged accuracy of proofs, there was no need to consult them on anything except whether they were both free to attend the book-launch. With an approach like this, word can get around. The printer is something of a tyrant in the print-shop, a matter which can make things better or worse depending on your outlook if it is also avowed that the printer is good at what he or she does. When the printer is also a poet, and relies upon others to publish their work, then this kind of reputation can be very useful. In my case, publishers have asked me if I wanted to design the book, or if there was anything I wanted them to be particular about, or if I would comment on their designer's work, and of course I have done all of these. In the beginning of my publishing life, I accepted the chance to design the books. The publishers seemed to think I'd do a good job, and what's more, it wasn't going to cost them anything. But in recent years I have pulled back from that amount of control over the work of others, and have wanted instead for the publisher to simply incorporate my writings into their programs in their own ways and by their normal process. The only stipulation I insist upon is that the design, thruout the book & its cover, be asymmetric on every page. It is then up to the publisher's designer to produce the goods and my experience to date is that they do.

¶ In 1996 the Holloway Press at the University of Auckland issued a limited edition of a Kendrick Smithyman poem, *Tomarata*. There are two unusual points about its printing. First is that, at that time at least (I have not been able to examine the rest of his archive), the poet used no spaces after punctuation within the line. Therefore, as a matter of course, I set the type accordingly. The first lines of section 9 thus look like this:

Open,to experience that satisfying
feeling of what goes unexplained.
Also,of continuity.True is when
whatever was hidden is revealed.
(Our language will not cope well
with reflexives.)It reveals itself
. . .

Even in the 1970s, when this poem was composed, the practice was not unique. It ought not have fazed therefore either magazine or book editors and publishers who have since relentlessly inserted word-spaces where there are none in the text. The limited edition I printed is thus the only occasion I know where this poet's practice has been observed in print. In my view there is no excuse whatever that can justify such rewriting of a poet's work. Another great New Zealand poet, Ursula Bethell, has also typed without word-spaces after punctuation within the line and, as far as I am aware, those works have never been published as written. Our editors and publishers have suffered here from a kind of collective cowardice and irresponsibility over many decades in this regard. When I wrote a number of works during the 1960s and 1970s that exhibited this practice, my interest in it lay in seeing that all the words were an equal distance apart and that punctuation was simply slotted into the spaces those equal distances allowed.

The second point is somewhat different, as the poet's own expectation would probably have been that publishers would print his work in a single color — black. Smithyman, thruout his life, composed mostly at the typewriter and during the time of the writing of Tomarata he used a two-color typewriter ribbon — red and blue. The poems were in blue and the section or part numbers were in red. The Holloway edition preserved this distinction and indeed reproduced two pages of Smithyman's typescript in the same colors beside the typeset text.

A nice articulation of my argument comes from a historian whose field is the book, Helmut Lehmann-Haupt. In a letter to Cummington Press printer Harry Duncan, Lehmann-Haupt wrote that the author may be 'through his creation of the sentence structure, through his paragraphing and through his use of the dialogue . . . the real book designer'.

¶ When poet Susan Howe composes work in which lines of type do not necessarily range one below the other in parallel lines, the precise angles and intersections of those lines are determined by the typeface and type-size she employs. What happens spatially to her texts when a magazine or book editor decides to set them in a different type. In conversation with me, she agreed that such reworking amounts to rewriting and that no amount of self-justifying talk about 'house style' can gainsay it. If the text is to be printed offset, then the author's disk can be used to transfer the precise image onto any page layout program. If the text is to be printed letterpress then the photopolymer plate is the perfect medium. Some poems are so exact in their spatial arrangement that the transfer from one type to another has the same effect as translation to another language — the original is lost in the attempt to reproduce it.

There was a time, in America primarily but also elsewhere, when many poets took great care over 'the disposition of words upon the page'. This phrase belongs to Stanley Morison, and he was referring to typography. But the syntactic arrangements of e.e. cummings and the typographic layouts of Charles Olson were precise organisations of their poems conceived as physical matter, much in the way a musical score is organised, or a calligramme by Apollinaire, or a typographic layout by Iliazd. Susan Howe's readings of Emily Dickinson are reliant on a fidelity to text that even the attempts of R W Franklin to accurately transcribe Dickinson's *Master Letters* from handwriting to print fail to measure up to. It is not that Franklin's failure is a miserable one, but looking at the facsimiles tells me that there are more options available on my word processor than were utilised by him, to the text's disadvantage and, therefore, to our disadvantage also.

❡ If one is writing a sonnet, one knows beforehand about where lines begin and end within that form. If one is writing poems that do not have such a predetermined form, then the question about where one line ends and another begins can assume singular importance, not only in relation to the work at hand, but to one's entire poetic praxis. Poems are works in which separate decisions are made about the lengths of the lines, whereas prose has no such issue. Thruout the twentieth century many poets, Pound, Williams, Ginsberg, Creeley, Olson among them, had fresh and clear ideas about how the line of poetry could be understood. The exact placement of lines, words, punctuation on the page was to act as something like a musical score, the placement telling us how the work was to be read.

The placement and its exactitude also tells anyone how it should appear in print. For poets who found in the typewriter a method of controlling their line-lengths and laying down strict spatial relationships with other lines, getting published in magazines and books could often, even usually, interfere with those relationships. The typewriter has each letter occupying the same width on the page, but typesetting has each letter occupying its relative width on the page. In the translation from one to the other, all the internal and external spatial connections and disconnections of the letters making up the poem were altered. A poem shaped in a circle for example on the typewriter could not be the same shape in typesetting unless the internal word-spacing was simply enlarged &/or narrowed to fit. And the same applies in the translation from one typeface to another typeface, long after the typewriter has ceased to be a generally accepted writing tool for the poet. At a time when the technologies of typesetting and of page layout can permit a near absolute fidelity to a poet's text as the basis for any given book design, it can seem astonishing that magazine editors (particularly those who are also poets) and book publishers so seldom take the opportunity. What amounts to an occasional exception in this regard ought to be the industry standard. The old letterpress typesetting adage 'Follow copy, even if it flies out the window' should be our most earnest as well as our highest endeavour as editors, printers and publishers of poetry. Book design then becomes an exercise in providing a context (there can be many of them) in which such 'following' can be made manifest.

¶ The question now is : When I would not let poets into my book design process, what am I doing asking other printers to accept direction from me when they print my texts. Well, it was always my intention to take the text, its line-lengths (there is no excuse for 'turn-overs') and spacing, as the absolute basis for the design. Only once or twice have I failed to put a new poem on a new page, and I have regretted those failures ever since. I also put too much word spacing in my earliest printed books but I quickly changed that. The point, however, is clear : the text is the Text.

In approaching other fine printers, I have approached only those for whose work I already have a deep respect. That means that for all those matters that I cannot or may not 'direct' I trust them. In fact, all I have asked for is two things : that the whole design be asymmetric, and that careful attention be paid to spacing in the crossover from one type to another. If a printer was unhappy with the first, then I would simply withdraw the text and try to place it elsewhere. I'd never argue with a printer who is used to doing things their way in their own printery. On the other hand, as a printer I would return a text to the author if the author made too demanding a direction against my own practice.

It is therefore a question of the limits of insistence, the limits of licence, and the sometimes fluid yet often clear dynamics between them. And my guess is that it is finally a matter of decorum, of how we are with each other in the context of our knowing : our knowing about text, our knowing about print, our knowing how to say yes and no to each other with good grace, whatever the risks. For myself, letting printers have their own licence has to date resulted in wonderful and utterly different fine books in limited editions. In each, the poems are beautifully shown, and remain themselves even tho the books are radically different from each other. It is a privilege one needs to learn : how to respect and how to direct the limits of insistence and the limits of licence.

2

Zephyros : the book untitled

this, tho I'll never know what 'this' will mean, is a book of the
book. Not 'the' book, nothing quite that elevated, quite that
hubric, but 'a' book, perhaps 'this' one. A book among countless others, derived from other books and delivered to them.
For whatever its claims, overt & covert, open & secret, its fate,
even if it came to be the Book of all books — that worst fate of
all — is to be, even simply, one book beside the others

a book is of & from a world
but the world is not a book
and a book is not the world

a book is not a man or a woman
or a child or a god of any kind

let the dictionaries bring all the words
back down to earth

let him write with a partial
and an impartial hand

=

to turn the page is to consign the previous page to memory
& forgetting. Mnemosyne is the inseparable double-take of
Lethe & Memoria, Greek & Latin, twin ghosts who haunt him
in the sunlight
                        opening the book
in hunger for the Nothing that he always, and never, finds

=

the utter necessity for a Muse of Astronomy, Urania. She is the
context in which all other Muses have their realms, in which
all earthly things take place — cosmos — sun, moon, & stars

=

one can never get out of the library in order to write. This is
not merely a metaphor. Its literal force is that all printed/writ-
ten books are around you, from your own small collection out
to all other libraries on the earth

=

a reading posture / a reading imposture
        away from the book, it does not stray from you

the book will not approach you
   nor will it abandon you
you cannot reach the book
   nor thrust it from you

=

distinctiones   the space between words
                      the space between lines
                      the space between pages
                      the space between books
                      the time between readings
                      the time between writings
                      the time between memories
                      the time between forgettings

=

the Eurydice effect — things do not disappear because you
turn away from them
                but because you turn *to* them

=

the music of the spheres
the murmur of language
the company of birds
the forest of leaves
the array of books

=

emptying the circle / emptying the head / emptying the heart
everything that is the case is in a state of flux
turning to this book or that book the Book disappears
it is not possible to bring the Book to book
thought flows as ink from the pen
emptying the book

=

the library, closed books on open shelves
the visible world — the material unconscious

turning the head
opening the book
turning the page
opening the heart

=

paper = white dust   humans = red dust

=

burning the books
burning the culture
burning the people
burning the Book

=

listen
over all the earth
to all the pages turning
floating in air

an endless rustle
& flutter
of leaves

=

YIN BOOK		YANG BOOK	
paper-bound	soft	hard	case-bound
open	hand	fist	closed
silent reading	inhale	exhale	declaiming
memory	roll back	press	future
shelf/personal	pull	push	altar/public
polylogue	cooperation	assertion	monologue

=

there is, hopefully, no Book to come. But the Book is merely
the idea of the book, not the book itself, and not the ideal, and
the books to come are legion

legio = a choosing, a chosen body, books as militia, with these
little soldiers of lead
we will conquer the world

=

'in the beginning was the World' — the so-called Word came later

to ob-literate/ob-liberate all other words that might make a
claim within us. It is a historical matter of power, not a mys-
tical one of poetry. The same applies to all other books that
would be the Book

books are made. They fall apart

=

a word went off in search of a book

a book of birds. a book of trees. a book of air. a book of earth

another book of birds. another book of trees. another book of air.
another book of earth

winged words

=

the spirit moving on the face of the waters, a mere puff of
wind that would destroy us all — *zephyr*

cloaked, you might say, in a book

=

the end of the Book, I long for it.   the end of the book is
nowhere in sight

all the ten thousand things are nowhere, in sight

=

nothing in the West corresponds to the Zen saying
'if you meet the Buddha on the road, kill him'.
And is that the fate of the West, to allow the Impostor
to roam free among us. The West still can't quite
believe that all gods are false

Herakleitos : 'the known way is an impasse'

=

in open air, read only those leaves turned by the breeze
the book to come   the book to go

=

ΖΕΦΥΡΟΣ —   god of west wind
                 light infantryman
                 soft breeze

light gauze shawl or shirt
butterfly
messenger of spring

3

Each new book

¶ each new book removes all others from view, but some will make themselves 'present tho absent' in memory. Repeated over a life this adumbrates — Skeat : 'to shadow forth' — a life's reading list, which underlies & overlays every new act of reading. Each new reading reasserts, modifies, or rejects, previous readings

the ancients, Plato for instance, who opposed reading/writing to memory, had not lived for long enough with reading/writing *and* memory to live in their intimacy, their interdependence, their deep &/or dire need for each other, the symbiosis that required a historical development to emerge

expunge all religiosities from the register — 'in the beginning was the word' a hubric rubric if ever there was one. The earth does not care what foolishness we adopt to exercise power over other books, other selves if 'secular' is of this age or generation, it comes from a root meaning 'to sow'. The seeds we sow that generate the world of & for others. Karmic, in the best sense, of the effect of what we do upon what happens to us — in 'this' life

is it really so, extrapolating Hegel via Blanchot, that the book is for us 'a thing of the past'. But is not the making of art, the life of being in the process of art, always a thing of the present, no matter the antiquity of whatever is at hand or before the mind. Only one not an artist could relegate or delegate art to 'a thing of the past'

¶ how may I understand this — over all the planet millions of words in unrelated & related languages are at this moment not being read, and many won't be. What words can be uttered about these words. Can 'words' even be a proper term for them. What holds these collections of words together other than the codices they're written/printed in and the shelves they stand or lie upon. We say of someone that they are still 'on the shelf', they are yet to be chosen by another, to be activated in various social senses. Myriad flowers, insects, fish, grasses are not seen, yet that they are there and have their own histories we take to be undeniable. Are unread words like that. Out of sight, into mind. Each volume has its small history, even if, after its manufacture, it was unsold & destroyed by its publisher. Yet to say of unread words or books that they are merely 'unread' seems insufficient

the inertia of the book

I once had a small 'vision', triggered by seeing television coverage of a large crowd in a sports arena. The overall vocal effect of the crowd was of a vast jumble of sounds in which no particular word or even syllable could be separately detected. When the camera zoomed in on a small group within the crowd, the sound one heard was still that of the crowd. I suddenly imagined that each of the persons within this isolated ensemble and, by implication, all other individuals in the crowd, was making the precise vocal jumble of unintelligible noises audible from the crowd itself. This may well have been my first experience or at least inkling of the idea of the murmur of language. People speak, crowds murmur, yet every intelligible individual's speech is a component in the crowd's unintelligible murmur. This is no doubt the outer form of the internal ('out there') murmur of language. Over earth, the murmur, the whole human murmur, cannot be heard, and the whole collection of printed/written words cannot be seen. They can, therefore, never be fully experienced. They can only be imagined or implied or extrapolated from other experiences. The murmur is a site in which every possible assertion will find its expression, its modification, its denial, its contrary. In the blur of printing/writing, we will find the same. How would it be if every such assertion were to make the same claim on someone. Impossible, of course. But if it were possible, would that someone ever be able to discriminate anything within the 'ten thousand things'

¶ I am unable to take the book on trust. That any book might trust me is an intolerable proposition positing the murmur is lifting the noise of speech away from speaking. It joins all other noise, wind in trees & grass, birds, traffic, sea-sound, the noise anything makes when it moves or breathes or stands in the way of other movement. Noise of the earth, earth-sound, neither music nor language, nor even anything specifically human. It has long been time to demystify and deprivilege our role/position in the so-called scheme of things

what if, haunted by a book, one's haunted not by any of its content, but by its form. This has certainly been my tendency, since childhood, when I wanted books but almost never read them. Even now I rarely read a book from cover to cover

¶ by what lore is the book bound. The anxiety of those, for instance, who find it hard to cope with paper bound books whose leaves break off from the brittle glue of their manufacture. Such a breaking off, a falling out, rarely elicits a neutral response. Why don't 'they' do it better, or properly, or differently so the book stays together. If a book simply falls apart, its leaves separated & scattered by historical process, then we can regret it while understanding how it happened. But to split the book up deliberately for personal, pecuniary advantage is usually to provoke as much outrage as understanding. Something terrible has happened in this instance, but what, exactly. The sale of separated leaves from rare books has more than conservational consequences

the terms often used for well-written well-bound books include 'magisterial', 'authoritative', 'definitive', 'the last word' etc, all proposing a judgment unlikely to be altered, a text not to be surpassed, and a virtual prohibition against any but the most trivial questioning. But take one of these solid tomes and rip out some of its pages, burn some, trash some, sell some. The book's life & flow in the world is interrupted. Its progress from one authoritative page to another, one generation to another, has broken the lore & law of the bound book. For the book to be binding for us, its binding must cohere. For us to remain at liberty in the book, the book itself must be chained to its determining institution, first in the library (Alexandria e.g.), later in the West the church, and now again the library, personal & public. Readers too will seek this kind of authority saying, 'I've read this book from cover to cover', as if that alone guaranteed a right to speak, when in fact the right to speak comes from another quarter. It's no surprise that the repeated re-renderings of the notion of the book since the late nineteenth century have been both authoritarian and anti-authoritarian in character

is it that the bound book is thus, being bound, captive to itself. Unbound, sheets can be added or removed, having the possibility of fluidity, or becoming something other than it is at any moment. We seek liberation in an object necessarily bound in chains

¶ the books of Giovanni Mardersteig imply a conservative acceptance of the traditional form of the book. He introduced no innovations to book design or structure, as if he simply wished to make trade books of an unusually high quality. His

Alphabetum Romanum is special because of its hand-coloring and because many of its pages are based on a fifteenth century hand-written manual for forming capital letters. But in all other respects, the designs of title page, preliminaries and the textual *mise èn page* are all conservative, recognisable and familiar to those whose main reading is of trade books. Was he, in spite of his great skill as a handpress printer, his flair at bringing disparate authors & artists together on the page, a *publisher* who used the handpress as his primary mode of manufacture. In a not dissimilar way, Blanchot's notion of the book is equally conservative. He takes no account of the transformations of the form & structure of the book as practised by fine printers and book artists thruout the century of his own writing

while many such transformations of the form of books have been termed 'violent', 'transgressive', 'hybridic', 'boundary-breaking', these terms have been much used by critics & commentators in contemporary letters without, as far as my knowledge goes, ever questioning the legitimacy of the terms. But many workers in the field do not see it as an 'attack', and less as a violence to the book. Instead they see an intimate, however radical, extension of the possibilities presented by the traditional form of the book, possibilities which inhere in the conservative structure of the book itself

¶ the term 'book' tends to acquire different kinds of response according to who wrote it and how the writer is regarded by the reader. 'My favorite author' and 'my favorite book' have often been used interchangeably, yet it tends not to be the physical book that is revered, unless the edition is a rare or limited one, or the reader has emotional attachments to a specific volume because it was a gift or an heirloom or came to them in childhood, or any number of such events. What is primarily favored is the experience of reading, whatever other affective context might have been operative at the time, and this separates particular volumes from the plethora of volumes that are gathered into the library, private or public. But the library, &/or the bookcase, houses books of widely different, even violently opposed, opinions, cultural assumptions, positions taken, and so on. What is our position in relation to the dynamic which contains such a collection of oppositions — without taking on any particular position or opposition that the writings express

when I write, it's a private matter. When I publish, it's a public matter, and the question of ownership is thrown open. I can own a copy of 'my' published book, but I can no longer claim ownership of the role that that book henceforth has or develops in the community. This of course has nothing to do with copyright

each day, each moment, the forest of trees, the array of leaf, looks different thru the same windows in the 'same' room in which I write. Each day the same books on the same shelves in the same room will be slightly different as individual volumes are taken from and replaced on the shelves. 'On my shelf' the book is not operative, but the same 'title' could be being read by another elsewhere. All this seems trivial enough at first and, perhaps last, glance. But how do we understand the library, I mean the world-wide collection of libraries, as more than a mere repository of volumes

let me take the word 'library' to mean the totality of volumes on shelves, public and private

what is it to take, apparently simply, a volume from a shelf

the unread library is in a state of flux

¶ choosing from the plethora — I remember vividly as a child standing in a public library being unable to choose a book, for how could I possibly choose from options that I did not know. Since then, I don't think I have ever taken from a library shelf a book whose author was not already known to me in some way, even if it were simply by recommendation from another person or another book

never read a book, she sd, without a pen & notebook beside you

never write a book, he sd, without a printed or written book beside you

the context of my writing is the plethora of printed/written books — the library

¶ the book has long since marked itself from being mere- ly a device for reading. It is no longer, as it were, 'the finger pointing to the moon'. Another saying — 'the map is not the territory' — is a partial truth only, and the partiality is only ever a matter of degree. The map has itself been part of the territory since the beginning of writing, the earliest inscriptions on stone or clay

that a piece of writing might be true for all times & places is likely to be simply a function of the beliefs of a particular culture or strand within a particular culture, whether a Shakespeare sonnet or any of the so-called 'sacred' texts. I/we believe it, therefore everyone else should believe it also. Yet I too have been under this illusion, that as a poet or commentator I could make 'true' remarks which could remain intact, Pound's 'the poet standing by their word', no matter who said them in whatever context. And this text here is one in which I am trying to make up sentences — 'is this true or did you just make it up' — by which I or anyone else might stand. Testimony, then, that might be altered, modified or overturned by further testimony — 'true enough'

¶ contrary to fashion, the space of reading/writing is not virtual, but real. It happens here & there, precisely, and always in time, always in a body

'trying to remember', then 'o yes, such & such'
'trying to forget' is not a parallel activity
remembering/forgetting is asymmetric
'I never think about it these days' does not mean 'I have forgotten'
One cannot try to forget, then succeed. Forgetting is not transitive

could one say 'there are no truths fixed for all time' — even this one. But, testimonies there are, which need continued testing by one's thought & experience. Keep thinking & writing & talking, and new sentences will emerge

might the book as repository of 'truth' be a lie that can only be covered up by the assertion of divinity. No god = no divinity. Even so, is it even possible at this stage to read the so-called sacred texts as 'literature', without taint of their 'divine' flatus

is 'giving a sentence one's assent' the same as 'this sentence is true'. Obviously not. Is 'giving a word one's assent' the same as 'this word refers to something real in the world'. Not at all

in the array of words there will be, in any language, a fair quantity of nouns which do not name anything actual in the world — a noun, in the parlance of one's school lessons, is not necessarily a naming word. What, on earth, does the word 'book' name

to say 'tree' is to reveal & conceal the fantastic variety of trees. Is it the same of 'book'. For by 'book' some mean 'text', or 'story', or 'reading experience', or 'physical object'. Not everyone means all of these

the problem with the 'book cultures' is not that they have a book as their basis, but that they have privileged their book above all others — the Book — erecting exclusivity within their identities, and devaluing the Other, which means 'all other books', 'all other persons'

¶ before me is a book printed wholly in Greek, that I can with difficulty pronounce but cannot read — what a thing of beauty it is. In this sense 'beauty' is possible by an abstraction away from content

a double life — leaf of the book / leaf of the tree
turning the head — to the desk / to the window

a triple life — book leaf / tree leaf / Dasein

squaring the triangle — book leaf / tree leaf / Dasein / cosmos

as with thousands of other species, human life had a beginning, and will have an end. Some say our thought elevates us above other beings, some say we are no different from other beings, tho consciousness remains a problem. In any case, the book is a puny device in the face of universal energy, the unimaginably explosive sort that generates galaxies over vast space and vast time. The exclusive Books are therefore doubly ridiculed, doubly beside the point

'there is no transcendental signified' / 'there is no transcendental book'

'what can I say' — not, 'what do I mean'

¶ when I recite the poem aloud, among others, I am the bard. The bardic process is thus a communal one, as the poetic process is a private one. The poet writes, the bard utters, is that it. But reciting is neither speaking nor reading. Perhaps 'recite' should have a more specific place in our thinking. The reciting bard as the public role of the private poet

it is not possible to bring the Book to book / 'more books' = 'more clutter'

the bardic recitation of the written poem is the link I have been looking for with Illich & Sanders' 'pre-alphabetic bard'. The bard remains the bard whether pre- or post- alphabetic. Obviously I have been using 'poet' and 'bard' promiscuously for each other

¶ the destruction of books, whether by publishers emptying shelves of unsold stock, or families of deceased estates tidying up after the death of a relative, is a regular, even daily, occurrence thruout the western world. However regrettable some of these instances are, they are nevertheless part of the normal state of affairs. If books and papers are thus burned, it is merely that this conflagration — imagine all the everyday burning/destruction of books & papers round the world happening at this moment — solves a fairly common problem. When the world ends — life of all kinds as we know it ends — the question of how anything was destroyed will not be able to be asked, and the means, whether burning or dumping or recycling, will be irrelevant. Is it possible that burning books of value, social, cultural, monetary, acts as metaphor for some intimate knowledge we all have of the final end to human life on earth, and our revulsion for book-burning comes from an unwillingness to be reminded of it

¶ here is one way of looking at it — there is a traditional Chinese view that it is a crime to destroy a book. A book has chi. All the crafts that go into making a book, paper-making, ink-making, calligraphy, drawing, printing, binding, are individually revered within the culture. To destroy them is to destroy what everyone reveres. The book contains both the expressiveness and the energy of its making and of its maker. It is a mark of the cultivation & achievement of its creators regardless of whether it holds any interest for others or to later generations. Passed on generationally, the book registers the attainment of knowledge thru the suffering and the craft of the individual, which is then given over to the rest of humanity. How shall I embrace — it's already within me in some measure — the Chinese view and avoid the taint of the 'sacred object'. What's the difference between a sacred object and a fetish object. Is it a see-saw of communal/personal

for some reason, and I have handled hundreds, even thousands of them, the two piles of hand-cut handmade paper on my bench this morning are beautiful to me — very beautiful, as if I had suddenly understood after all this time that it is paper that makes a book, and more so than type or words or images. It's an odd event for someone in my position to be sure, but it is certainly what it feels like this morning under a blue sky after night's rain with silver drops highlighting myriad leaves

what is it that elevates or distinguishes one item in the world of items as having symbolic value. Gold instead of excrement. Retention instead of letting go or evacuation. What have higher and lower orders to do with the ten thousand things. The ten thousand things are not to be discriminated. All things 'as is, where is', no high or low, saved or wasted, loved or hated, kept or lost

¶ if all is no more than a cycle of birth & death, then why conserve anything

while I do separate one book from another in terms of value, how is it that I also separate 'book in general' from other general categories of object for specific attention. Is my 'choice' more than a simple function of the conditioned nature of things

in relatively closed communities what comes to have symbolic value is decided historically by the community itself, almost independently of the individuals who constitute that community. Where the community is relatively open, there's increasing scope for its individuals to make symbolic value decisions for themselves

is it possible that in not taking x as having symbolic value we do not also have to actively reject or devalue it. Certainly people do assign negative symbolic value to things, acts &

social practices. But can we have a neutral approach to all those things, acts & social practices we decide not to positively value. Could you take 'jargon' as a positive value, a term of material description, without burdening it with the pejorative

these words : value, symbolic, transcendent — all lift away from or add something to the neutrality of the ten thousand things

'the book, spiritual instrument' // 'the book, material instrument'

the book as an operational term as well as an ontological one (recalling from *Sidetracks* — 'a noun is a doing word'

¶ most editions are an excess, and often remaindered. Perched on a shelf, books are the product or dross of a process, from writing to manufacture, driven by social practices, from publishing to generation of income. The focus, along either of these axes, will vary according to the primary values of those involved, but the spectra are fairly stable. How do we speak of those books we will never open again. A remainder, 'a mordant residue', as someone once put it, a trace (as in 'whatever touches anything leaves a trace'

if a book is issued in several editions, each with 'additions & alterations', we cannot assume that the subsequent editions have a positive or improved value. We can critique them as readily as we can the first edition, and that is often done in reviews. But there can be many reasons for preferring a first edition to a revised one, and some of those reasons can be extrinsic to the perceived quality of the text itself. That a particular edition came to one as a gift from a loved relative is a good example of a book having extrinsic value, even if the text itself might not have been particularly gripping. Limited editions are invested, worthy of it or not, with an added value intrinsic to their making. But the question of the value of discarded volumes, the unread, even unreadable library, is still an issue, and the sorts of intrinsic & extrinsic values I have been pointing to do not seem to me to apply to them

'remaindering' is the name of a process that attempts to revive a title not fully sold. Once remaindered the book is offered for sale at a lesser price in the hope it will enter the stream of book ownership and thus cease being a remainder. In this sense, all unsold books can be seen as remainders. An author's 'remains' are those writings, in whatever form, not published at the time of the author's death. Published, they cease being remains, and the original papers can either be destroyed or made into an archive. An archive can thus be read as a collection of remains that can be rekindled by the attention of readers. The unread library can be rekindled also by the attention of readers. It costs a lot of money and social effort and expertise to maintain these remains and the unread library. The prospect of destroying or burning them is still profoundly unacceptable to most people, but what if they are *never* read

when we learn of the holocaustic destruction of the great library at Alexandria, apart from its role as a power-play by an exclusive culture attempting to obliterate another culture, it is easy to feel a sense of loss when we are told that countless ancient philosophical, historical, scientific and literary texts were taken from later generations in that fire. How different is that destruction from the collected volumes of the unread library which no one will ever read again

¶ would it make sense to imagine the unread library as a kind of material unconscious. Words & images lying fallow that could erupt into awareness at any time, not only from our life of dream or creative reverie, but also from the material external world itself. Words & images that were once conscious and are now — ah, the words are 'suppressed/repressed', but that's the active repulsion/rejection I wish, for a while at any rate, to avoid. Remaindered? But remainders are books a publisher is trying to put into circulation. Is it simply that 'remainder' has a double edge : remains (what is not in circulation) / remainder (what is about to be circulated)

is it circulation. The unread library is out of circulation, yet has the potential for being re-circulated at any time. And as this does occur, the unread library is not stable as to its composition. Items in the unread library are as retrievable as items in the active library. In second-hand book stores, public & private libraries, the unread & the active libraries are often perched on the same shelves

I have been hearing 'dead' in 'unread' in these notes. But there is clearly a dynamic between these twin libraries that keeps

the prospect open that any part of one can become part of the
other at any time

when images, words, narratives come to consciousness in dreams
when images, words, narratives come to consciousness in books
the one process is immaterial, ephemeral
the other process is material, long-lived
the one has gone forever
the other can be returned to ad infinitum

presumably, if the unread library is a twin within the dynamic
of the unread/active library, it is, to that extent at least, alive.
To burn the books is to burn something that is still alive, and
the 'something' is also alive within human beings. Burning
books, burning people, the same

books as a mode of access to the collective, conscious &
unconscious

¶ reading as a purely private activity — I can no longer believe
it. It is so of writing also. In libraries — reading is public. In
my home — reading is public

if I close a particular door in the house, my partner knows
I am writing and will not therefore interrupt me. It is a
kindness she offers me within the dynamics of our social
interactions. Externally, writing is thus a function/factor in
our relationship. Internally, how does it stand. The words I
write were given to me in/by the community in which I grew

up and are, by publication, given back to the community again, tho not necessarily to the specific area of community in which I grew up. I have, as they say, moved a long way away from that. Edward Said's word 'affiliative' is deeply affective for me in this context. My apparent withdrawal from community in order to write is therefore a function of my relationship with that community, tho any notion from the 'cultural studies' puritans that that is all it is, has to be rejected with all the strenuousness one can muster

¶ making the unconscious conscious. Max Gimblett's skull-forms spread about the floor = low tide. Allen Curnow also saw that low tide was a revelatory process, uncovering the hidden, and a life-long concern — sailing/drowning, passage to the other shore

Lew Welch : Guard the mysteries!
               Constantly reveal them!

Sappho/Barnard : If you are squeamish
                  Don't prod the
                  beach rubble

we talk/write about the unconscious, do we not, as if all its contents are of deep and necessary significance. What if the unconscious, whatever its genuine importance, yet contained vast quantities of rubble. Is it necessarily gold, just because it came from there is there anything complete about a book. A thing finished and a thing done, are they the same. I can return to a published book and pick up something to develop or expand into new writing. In Max Gimblett's journals he returns to 'completed' volumes and adds to them, however minimal the new gesture. These volumes are in a constant condition of potential incompletion, and fresh marks can be added many years after the initial event. In a published edition the flow of marks is halted. But what was it that made of W H Auden & Kendrick Smithyman e.g. the tinkerers they were, who rewrote again & again after publication

¶ from the vantage of production, individual volumes are remains of a process that is not used up by the sale of the edition. The rivers of printed matter are pouring out of print shops of every description, effluvia in every sense. We even say, we are 'dipping' into a book, as into a moving stream

all my interest in books, or my main interest in books, has been in what most people regard as the least significant aspects, that is, everything aside from reading

tho I open several books each day, tho I am surrounded by books, books I own, books I use, books I refer to & defer to, books I write, books I collect, what I most decidedly do not do, is read a book

do I only ever think on the page, as Wittgenstein has it, 'thru the pen' the writings of Blanchot on the book come from the depth of his life/work as a reader. Can it be said that I enter the discussion from 'the other end', as if it were a genuine spectrum. He enters the finished book/text, I enter the process of a text in its becoming a book. Whatever I lack by staying on my side of the spectrum, and I know some who'd say I therefore lacked everything because I do not read, is what I gain on this side enough for me to talk about the whole thing. Maybe that lack is crippling, deforming, in my case. Often, it certainly seems so to me. Could something therefore similar be said about the profound text orientations of Derrida, Blanchot, and Jabès. If so, it should not be imagined that I am thereby diminishing their achievements, or mine, for that matter

¶ there is no doubt that fine press books propose a value for their material existence per se. This value could be seen as a replacement/rejection of the 'spiritual' value of the 'sacred' object. This is not merely the slip of my prejudices showing (tho I do not deny it is that) but also the whole undergarment in contrast to the invisible threads by which the 'sacred' has bound communities together against other communities. The chosen book is the chosen community, even in the avant garde. The question remains — how do I value the book without rendering it 'sacred' — even if the sacred is read simply as 'a thing apart'

presumably, the 'ideal' does not have to have a fixed form

it's clear I am seriously ek-centric. I live far away from all

forms of large collective *behaviours* — crowds at the beach,
sports events, movie theatres, xmas or new year gatherings,
churches, street marches, institutional or club memberships
etc. Yet my own small and fairly private life is dependent upon
a fairly stable society

sometimes we use the term 'ideal' to signify something that
suits or fits us or a purpose to our satisfaction. 'It's ideal, just
what I've been looking for'. Ideal is 'best' or 'fit for purpose'
— a long way from Plato's Idea. The ideal is thus the conjunction of the idea and its realisation. The idea seeks the thing or
circumstance that renders it ideal

the Book seeks the book, and the book constantly feeds into
the idea of the Book
which seeks the book

the mob reads

¶ it is of great use to western governments that most of the
finest minds in their constituencies spend most of their time
& intellectual effort directed away from the abject failure of
those governments to legislate for a fair and decent society for
all its citizens — in my father's words, 'they've got their noses
stuck in a book'

us humans now have enough resources to feed, clothe, house,
educate and look after the health of everyone on the planet,
and we are not going to do it

to legislate is less to write the law than to change it. The law, and the books of the law, is not only in a state of flux but it differs radically, nation to nation. If the Law is the Book of the Law, then the laws will never reach it. If the Book is the Book of the Law, then the books will never reach it

how interesting it is, at least to me, that I set about expressing so many 'truths' in the form of an invalid proposition, $p \supset q$, i.e. if p, then q

¶ what are the prospects that a new Book would historically emerge. If the Books were burned, all of them, every book of the Books erased, what chance is there of a new Book springing to life. An unanswerable question no doubt. But the Books are historical creations, and if there's some, there may be more. Our capacity for self-delusion is limitless

what I do, in spite of my own delusional life, is replace the Book with books, plural. If I were however to make a definitive list of the particular books that are definitive for me, what then have I come up with

is it possible to dismiss the Book, say, The bible for example, and retain for oneself parts of the book, The song of songs for instance

the Book is definitive for those who live by it. All the multiple readability in the world will not change that for them. Those who live by the Book live within a horizon that is relatively fixed. Those for whom the Book is not operative live within a horizon that is relatively mobile. These levels of fixity and mobility parallel our range of capacity to accept others in their difference. My problem here is that I am very intolerant of those who are intolerant of others. The Book has everything to answer for in this regard

is it rather that there is always the Book, whether one values any Book or not. If my Book is an array of books and not a single Book, what does that do for the Book as a multiple secular working concept. When a book becomes an exclusive Book, it is the same kind of process as when a man becomes a god

¶ in the beginning was the cosmos and the word came a long time after. The other theory, that the word brings the cosmos into being, is another obfuscation. Better to remember Vico — the world creates the words and the words shape the world for us, but the cosmos was there long before the world

whatever happens on the earth, the earth has created. Our words are earthy, per se. Specifically dirty talk, rough & foul language, merely reminds us that all words, even the most high falutin, come out of the mouths of creatures made out of earth

any phrase, sentence, paragraph, picture or story from any book whatsoever is capable of striking the spark of thought. The unread library has this potential at all times. The very term 'potential' contains the spark of life, waiting to be enlivened. And in fact anything in the world has this potential also — *potentia*

¶ is there anything blank about a blank page, for mind & history are already exhibited & focused there, the blank page already palimpsest, covering up & bringing forth

we say, many of us who make books by hand, that we design a book thru our engagement with the text. I don't doubt that for many of us it is true. But for me it is far more usual that what stimulates the design is an engagement with the shapes of the text and the materials available for the work. Looking more than reading. Looking at more than looking thru. A dynamic between text shapes and materials & equipment from the start

we say that a work can exhibit one's signature, even if not signed. There is something indefinably there, sensed not seen, something one can't quite put one's finger on, but if you look at this or that etc

the human being, is it the same as 'gesture', in the work, inevitably, even if part of one's purpose is to create works that occlude any sense of gesture at all. But Vasarely, Albers, Riley etc are all astonishingly identifiable

only once did I print a book to another's design. Tho the process was entirely satisfactory — relations with poet, artist, publisher all one could ask, and the book very attractive to me — I determined never to do it again. It did not look as if it had come from my hands. My invisible signature was not visible to me there

I do not, or I am unable to, recognise the experience implied in this : 'when I write or read I am in another world'. I am equally unable to relate to those who say 'I love words', 'I love writing', 'I am an avid reader' etc

a signature is perhaps simply what is particular about a thing. It has to do with recognition & memory rather than signage. I have seen this unseeable mark before. No one else's brush mark looks like that, no one else's handwriting looks like this

I confess I do not trust a disembodied imagination. Writing is still the-work-of-the-body-in-the-body-of-the-world

¶ form of a cup.   form of a box.   form of a book.   What springs to mind

what would you make, if it were mortally put upon you, if you were required to invent a form that was not a book as we know it, but served that book's total function & purpose. To say 'computer' is to miss the point entirely

the book historically is a gathering of pages joined at one edge. The scroll is a gathering of pages joined at two edg- es. It is hard to imagine another possible form. It's possible that current alternative binding structures made by artists and binders, however far they genuinely reach from the tradi- tional form, are a recognition of this apparently adamantine circumstance. And whatever their achievements, and not in the slightest to diminish or devalue them, none of those alternatives could replace the traditional form as a matter of common manufacture

¶ the book as form, the book as volume, the book as text, the book as experience.

the form of the book is not maintained only by the difficulty of imagining/inventing a physical alternative, but also by the whole socio-economic apparatus, world-wide, involved in the production of them — the factory, and the storage of them — the library

it is still hard for me to accept that the book's form might have to be accepted as an unquestionable given. And as hard for me to depart from it

the invisibly fine line, possibly non-existent, between the provision of information and the attempt to persuade

¶ why would I write this for another to read. Everything I write, I have long said, is hopefully and already on the way to becoming a book. If I rarely earn any money from writing, then what sort of pressure's involved in wanting an audience. A large readership has never been my interest, yet without some readers no one will publish you. But I have a strong interest in getting published, and while my publications list is impressive, especially to me, very little has been written about it he has often seen publication as part of the writing process. Is he thus using publication as a private mechanism for getting from one work to another. Yet publishing releases the work from his ownership, regardless of copyright, and he has no further control of the book as it serves, one way and another, the community into which it is released

publishing = letting go

is publishing, for him, the perfect gift, from which he expects, desires, no return. He wants his small editions, trade & limited, to sell. He would like his work to be written up, as they say, in his lifetime. He has never been invited to participate in a writers festival, and knows he would decline any invitation to do so. He is one of the most regularly reviled poets in the country of his birth over some twenty-five years. He has no interest in being a 'household name' in letters. Yet what is publication for if it is not to be a publicly empty gesture performed for private purposes. It is certainly a considerable labor to put others to. Yet he still does not write without envisioning the book to come

there is an implicit obedience required of the reader. Is this why I rarely read — I refuse to obey

¶ if one were to give 'Book' fresh currency, could it be a renaming, or a retrieval of one of its myriad names, of the Trickster, Hermes, or Maui, who utters fact & opinion, truth & lies, in the single breath that is speech itself. Hermes is thus the human species, that speech itself hung somewhere between the human and the divine, between heaven & hell, between sky & earth, and the Word became severed from its proper human & multifarious dimensionality

Book, Word & Law are in flux because of their inextricable relations with book, word & law. Having come to being, they fold into each other, in constant conflict & interchange

¶ if Being is the being of entities, then Being too is in flux. Was this Heidegger's error, that for all his wonderful complexity & sensitivity, he wanted 'Being' to be a concept 'at one's disposal'. Those who value the exclusive Book want the same thing

'the book to come', Blanchot's resonant, redolent phrase, tho for him it is more accurately 'the text to come'. Can we desacralise the Book and retain the capital

the book to come. / the Book to go.

here, I let it go, it's your book, or world's book, or discarded book, or unread book, like the rest of them, and like these pieces offered up to the book, as Robert Creeley put it —

> Things
> >   come and go.
> Then
> >   let them.

4

What book does my library make

My own view is that you take these things personally. You do an experiment because your own philosophy makes you want to know the result. It's too hard, and life is too short, to spend your time doing something because someone else has said it's important. You must feel the thing yourself.

— Isidor I. Rabi

¶ I'd like to read my books. I have some, and I see their backs turned to me, daily. They are shelved, and not that many of them, across four parts of the house : the printery, the sitting room, the bedroom, the corridor. I see them all, every day, even if not one is opened, making me more acquainted with the spines of books than with their pages and the words and images disposed upon them. It is many years since I have read a book from cover to cover. To use an earlier trope from Beatrice Warde, I could almost say that in my desire for the wine of thought, feeling and something akin to an infinite conversation, I have instead collected a pile of goblets. But I am about to cease making books, and my thought turns to the books in the house, most of which are unread in any normal sense, tho I will have glanced at a page or two, here & there, in each of them. In some, I have looked only at their paratexts : titlepage, epigraph, endnotes, bibliography, index and so on. But to read a book — this has often seemed to me a presumption of power, a kind of violence, to read the words of another in their absence. Holding the book, stroking it, gazing at it, the very language of what we do with books proposes an intimacy, a permissiveness for which I at any rate have received no permission. As if some right has not been earned, some ritual of meeting has not been enacted, some invitation has been presumed simply because others have preceded me, some test of acceptability has not been passed. Are all of us who publish clear that anyone, anyone at all, might read us, whoever they are, whatever they have done, whatever they are likely to do. Do we really want our book in this or that person's hands. Many painters exercise a veto on their works being sold to certain people or institutions. And many writers and artists have seen the destruction of their works and at times lost their liberty or their life because their work came into unsympathetic hands. How do I dare to read or to write a book

¶ my library, for want of a better term, is not large. It has approximately one thousand volumes, and at my reading speed it would probably take me about forty years to read each volume once only, by which time I would be 110 years old. If I have actually only about twenty years left to me, you can see the problem. Perhaps I should extrapolate from Ezra Pound's recipe for a magazine : a core of regular writers around which a variety of others would come & go as the editor chooses. A set of core books as main text, with the others serving somewhat as paratexts, something like that perhaps. In any event I know I am not going to be able to read them all, and the small, fanciful part of my imagining asks what the library itself, and its authors, might think of that

¶ liberated from printing books, maybe now I can learn to read them

¶ at my age, how redolent is that empty phrase, there is a danger of sliding into a trope of petrification. The body's arteries are hardening, and are one's responses also. If I could settle for a few basic unshakeable truths for company, mellow with time and the cooling of the infant's rage turned to adult anger turned to an ageing crankiness. I have seen others do it, this reversion, this shrinking of personal scope and possibility, and I fear it, dreadfully, in myself. I know that this dread lurks behind my otherwise legitimate urge to learn to read and rethink my library

¶ late in the nineteenth century W W Skeat in his *Etymological Dictionary of the English Language* defined the word 'book' this way : 'a volume; a written composition'. Over the last few months I have become increasingly aware that many people, talking/writing about 'the book' slide back & forth between these apparitional binaries without being aware of what they are doing. It's a habit. It seems natural somehow that we use the term 'book' promiscuously for both codex & text, a volume

& a written composition, as if everything we could say about one, we could also, without further question, say about the other. The interesting thing is, I can't believe anyone is actually confused about the differences between the book-object and any text it might be seen to carry. And yet we do so often make statements about one that can only be made about the other, and I think this happens at some of the most sophisticated levels in the discussion. At perhaps the crudest level, if one said 'I have written a book, but it's not published yet', I'd want to say that one has actually said something about a text, and not about a book, for a text cannot be a book until it is published. Perhaps we need to reconnect with the idea that the codex is the only form we know of the book, and that other forms of textual transmission need names and thinking that distinguish them from the book, rather than conflate them with the book because 'textual transmission' is common to them all

¶ we also do it in a kind of reverse. Because we have discovered we can 'read' more things than a book, like the weather, nature, paintings, buildings, body-language, animal bones, yarrow stalks, timetables, rubbish dumps, product packaging, clothing, clocks, bus tickets, junk mail, fashion etc, perhaps we believe we are extending, enlarging, blurring boundaries, hybridizing, border crossing, liberating from puritanical conservatisms, democratizing the category of 'the book'. Perhaps we believe we are allowing a greater and more humane or humanizing understanding of modalities of transmission in more cultural contexts than that of the western book tradition alone. I don't have any argument with non-book, non-western modes of textual transmission or generation. But I wonder if referring to them as 'books' may unintentionally obscure their difference, elide their special reality and function in other communities and contexts, opt for assimilation of the other into our own categories for our purposes, and inadvertently determine for others the heading under which non-book readabilities shall be discussed. In an effort to accommodate a greater readability, we may in fact be shortening the list of allowable categories instead of lengthening it

¶ the book. the text. how stark the difference seems to me as I prepare to cease printing after years of (almost) not reading. To turn from the book to the text. I won't forget tho that as the book tends to disappear as one reads, so the text tends to disappear as one thinks. There is no way out of this indeterminacy. The head of Orpheus turns forever, and Eurydice endlessly returns to the dark

¶ what might it be like, never to buy another book. Do the library's arteries harden, or does even a small number of books resonate, inform, and keep you alert to the options for longer than a single life can be lived. Would I ossify if my library remained static, does a static library = static person, static writer. Doesn't it depend on what the books are and who is reading them, and how they are reading them. How long would it take, if one only ever read one book, for one's speech & writing to assume (however well or badly) the tonalities, flavors and grammatics of that one book. Would I end up writing like Wittgenstein for example who is surely lurking in the way I am posing the questions here

¶ mythologically the Muse comes to you and withdraws from you. There is it seems to me nothing to be gendered in her, she is neither female nor is a possible object of desire. We write, we paint, we dance, we do anything at all at the pleasure of an energy that has been personalised at the beginning of western high culture (however eastern and Dionysian its origins) as She. The Muses are thus She for both men and women, but if the Muses are a myth, then so is their gender. One could say that the Muse is merely a metaphor, a function of the way we use language, that has hardened like the arteries into a figure given form because that's what humans do when they talk about something in the same way often enough and for long enough. But what if one takes it differently, that the Muse is less of a mythological structure or story, less of the name of a personal or internal impetus to creative activity, who removes your responsibility for what you do, your agency for how you behave, but instead is one of the otherwise innumerable names of our relation in and with the world. What if, for instance, I proposed the Muses as The Library, the collection of books spread out all over the planet, a library that has no opening or closing hours, that we can never visit and never leave, and in which we inevitably and irrevocably read and write. The Muses give you the library to read and have first and last claim on your books when they are published. The Muse is the cradle, the museum, and the grave of our writerly activity, impulse and production, genesis and repository: MOUSEION, the ancient name for the home of the Muses and the name of the library at Alexandria that was intended to house all the books of the world. The Muses are the library of the world, and the Muse is the library of my own devising. The library comes to you and withdraws from you

¶ the hand that any of us have in shaping the library at large is miniscule. But the portion of the library that is my personal library, how has that been formed. What degree of agency have we exercised when we have been given books, bought books on others' recommendations, acquired books to teach or be taught by, have been sent books to review (some of which we would never have bought), we might buy a box of books to get the one out of the twenty-five in it we really wanted, we are occasionally disappointed in one of our own purchases, and so on. Yet while we don't always choose the books we have, we don't often go into a bookshop and say to the bookseller 'I'd like ten books please, of various sizes and various prices, to the total value of $300' and then let the bookseller decide which volumes we will take home. But this question and others like it have been following me about the house, that is, about my library, for several weeks. So, if the choice were mine, what books would I include in my library, and what of the present collection would I discard, knowing that, short of their destruction, discarded books still have a place in the library at large

¶ I have no interest in cataloging systems or other modalities of ordering, whether title alphabetic, author alphabetic, the color spectrum of covers, the height of codices, or subject matter etc. Not even the books I have printed over nearly 34 years are gathered in the same part of the house, or even in a special, say, glass-fronted bookcase for their protection. But the text/paratext notion mentioned earlier has been suggesting a re-ordering of my present books, along with a fresh set of decisions about whether, of any volume, I will ever open it

again. And with this comes another question, to be asked as if it were being asked for the first time : what is the purpose of my library, when the collector's primary interest in ownership is barely, in my case, operative. Vague categories begin to make themselves known — books to read, books to look at, books to refer to, books I have printed, books of my texts printed by others, is that it. To order a library in terms of what I might want to do with it. What is the dance to be done with the library in order to make both of us work. Yet I still do not have an answer to the question : what does it mean, to take a book from a shelf

¶ my library is what it is at 10.04 am on this Sunday morning, but beyond that temporal determination, the library has always been in a state of flux. In it the volumes come & go. At different times activity quickens in one or other part of it, and has slowed to a halt in other parts. Reading, or looking at, will happen variously at the dining table, in the sitting room, at the desk in the printery, sometimes on the train to & from the city, but never, in my case anyway, in bed. To follow the track that any book makes when it leaves the shelf and moves around the environment, gets handled in various ways, is to follow a path that is not quite our own. Yet, to what extent is the self we are tied to, part of, a function of, the shelf that books are tied to. At one time books were literally so tied or chained to the shelves that housed them. So is there no shelf or desk outside the library, no transcendental location for a book or for a self

¶ in the movement, constant, continuous, of books off shelves and back again, the identities of the people who accompany them are of what relevance. It's not that the books have 'a life of their own' (dancing with the toys when the lights go out), but as long as there are people who have to do with books, books will have this traveling life of small or large journeyings in which humans can seem little more than participatory factors

¶ what happens to your sense of your library if you lend a book, take five years pestering the borrower to return it, and when it is returned to you in the mail, you find the borrower has written their own name in the book in indelible ink. Whose book is it, exactly, especially if you never knew the story of how that particular name came to be in the book. You could easily and with justification assume that the book 'belonged' to whoever's name was in the book, and that the person in whose library the book was found was the borrower

¶ I never write my name in books, and I do not buy books with marks of ownership in them. There's something about such claims that goes against the grain for me. Marks of ownership make claims that cannot be substantiated. That many people spend good money for such marks, of ownership or association, is supplemental to the integrity of the volume. The bookplate particularly can be seen as an attack on the integrity of the art of the book, and on the freedom of reading

¶ picture your library, from the beginning of its life to the present, and see the coming & going of books on & off the shelves over the library's lifetime. In many cases, even the shelves will have moved, changed or been replaced according to personal circumstance. It may even have been merged with or separated from the libraries of others. I want, whether I come back to it or not, to keep this picture of books swarming in and out of bookcases over a lifetime firmly in mind as a fluxual context for all else that might be said

¶ whatever else a book as a work of art might be, it is still a thing, an object, a mere member of the ten thousand things

¶ a poem as fragment
  a book as fragment
  a library as a fragment of the library at large
  the library at large as a fragment of the galaxy
  the galaxy as a fragment of the cosmos
  what a puny thing it is, a book, a library, a shelf, a self

¶ can one's library ever be said to lack anything. Is it not already fullness, excess, overflow, beyond any possible current grasp. Does it not already outstrip you before a single volume is collected there. There are many reasons why volumes come

& go, yet I want to say that their present absence is not lack, because my library will always exceed my reach, and books absent from my library remain in the library at large

¶ we tend, do we not, to talk of texts as if they have no location in a fast-moving and extremely mobile world. We cannot talk of books like that. Each volume is always and ineluctably somewhere, even if that somewhere is incredibly mobile. Its location, in principle, can be tracked. But is the location of any book a neutral matter. And is a book's or a library's location supplemental to the otherwise concrete existence of the books themselves

¶ I have long heard and wanted to hear the phenomenological cry 'to the books themselves!' (I have it from Heidegger). It is for me less a considered philosophical position than an emotional one — it moves me, I respond positively to it. But looking at my library and wondering whether these are the books I want gathered there, is posing more questions than simply : is this to be my reading list

¶ when I went at age twelve to High School, one of the first things done by the English teacher was to hand out a sheet of paper to each student and say 'this is your reading list'. I vividly recall my complete bewilderment at this event and at this remark. And I am still trying to figure out what it means, and what that list might contain, and how it might come to be written

¶ when Mallarmé writes 'poetry is sacred' or that the book is a 'spiritual instrument', my own secular impulse does not set out to deny him his insight or to disagree with him. It is rather that such language as 'sacred' or 'spiritual' is of no resonant value for me. I simply, or complexly, have to find some other way of articulating the book's sometimes delicious, sometimes terrifying, sometimes banal, excess

¶ the book as the excess of text, text's supplement, D F McKenzie's 'the book itself is an expressive means'. The book is more than, extra to, the text. It has a history as bodily existence and function that is not that of the text. Going back to Skeat, the volume is a signifying supplement to the written composition. And yet this seems almost rudimentary, of course, hasn't one been listening etc

¶ but reading a text is excess to the volume. Volume and composition therefore are in excess of each other. Between them, the invisible slide from one to the other, the elided slide, 'slide here' says the door to the library, the lecture room, the bookshop, the academic essay, the organisation devoted to your subject where we are helplessly asked to leave our baggage at the counter. Yet it is clear that I have valorised one side of this apparent excessive equation over the other for over twenty years

¶ let me, without further explanation, ask whether the dictionary might be seen as text or as paratext, or both

¶ at any opening of a book, the rest of the book is closed. At any taking of a book off the shelf, all other books remain there. 'To focus is to avert the gaze'

¶ in some parts of Jewish religious practice, the scroll of the Torah is handled by and passed around the congregate in a kind of Hassidic exuberance, dancing and whooping with joy at the very existence of the scroll itself, a communal, celebratory dancing with the sacred volume. At a certain point everything slows down and the scroll is unrolled to its full length and set about as a circle, the joined pages supported in the hands of everyone there. The rabbi then goes from person to person and reads a small portion of that part of the scroll that each person is holding up. The entire text is visible all at once, and this is not something that can ever be done with a book. In this event, both sides of Skeat's volume/composition binary is attended to

¶ dancing with a secular book, is it possible. What volume would you choose, or what cluster of volumes. How could such a ceremony ever be carried out in and by a secular community in the face of the choices each person would actually make

¶ the bound book binds, the ravelled scroll connects, the secular books network in the flux of change & difference

¶ is the repositorial function of a library akin to the function of the unconscious — and how we have come to reify this metaphor over the years

¶ could we posit the book of nature, paperless, wordless, uncontainable in any library as the unconscious. We cannot know anything about the unconscious, yet there are millions of words uttered & written about its supposed form & function every week. We cannot know anything about the book of nature, yet there are millions of words uttered & written about it every week. Wittgenstein famously urged us not to speak of what we cannot know. Humans have generally ignored him, for perhaps nobody wants to be quite that reasonable

¶ my library does not belong to me, or, I can own a volume but not a composition, own a book, but not a text, not even a text of my own composing. Could we say : no border crossing between books and texts is possible, for if this were not so, one would have to deny that the principle of indeterminacy operates here. And yet there is a plethora of claims thruout the world of the book about blurring boundaries, extending borders, hybridization, category transgressions and so on every day. Do not these claims rely upon a fixity of category formation that was actually never true. The supposed edges of the categories always were straw edges, and the language of their apparent violent demolition was always a straw victory

¶ reading a book and reading a text is an example of indeterminacy. We cannot do both at once. There is instead a sort of shuttling back & forth (loom-shuttle, weaving, textura) however rapid, between the two. Even in the case of the books of William Blake. Is it simply that human attention is monocular, and our stereoscopic vision merely gives us a depth of field. And wouldn't being able to see both sides at once imply that our experience is atemporal, permitting us to transcend the detail, the particular, the contingent that would pin us down. But in any articulation of any experience we speak or write as anyone does, one word after the other, one word or element or object at a time. Unless one's understanding of time & succession is all wrong, and that 'one word at a time' is an inaccurate way of talking about how we talk and how we write. For at this point I remember that the writing of the ancient Greeks prior to the 5th century BC knew no word spaces. But looking at one word renders all other words in its vicinity almost invisible. Looking at an image renders the environmental context of that image invisible. Foreground/background, reading/viewing, focus/panorama, detail/overall impression, indeterminacy everywhere

¶ what single written composition does one's own library, one's own collection of volumes, make. What sort of a book is one's library. What book does the accumulated libraries of all of us amount to. Louis Zukofsky famously avowed that all one's life one only wrote one poem. It allows the nice possibility that all poems from a certain context, all L=A=N=G=U=A=G=E poems for example (let's allow for the moment that such things do exist), are a single poem, parts of which are distributed about various, diverse, even conflictual writers. It reminds me of a Terry Riley composition in "Cadenza on the Night Plain" where a Dream Collector has a specific and finite number of dreams to distribute and redistribute thruout the populace after collecting them from the dreamers in the morning. So the library at large, that collection of books scattered yet gathered over the planet, is itself a single book, containing a unitary text, the variety and complexity of which is unencompassable by any individual, any tribe, any nation, any book, even the entire populace, those millions who every day die and are born, dropping as a species, as it were, into & out of the text

¶ our individual libraries, our tiny collections of affirmative adhesions, are little more than our particular share in the general implication. However I may come to shape my personal library now, I have already been shaped by the unbounded & unbindable library at large

¶ if I think again of the unconscious as an external rather than internal structure, as the world/galaxy/cosmos, in which the library at large is merely a small component, the unconscious, that is, out there rather than in here, then it is not difficult for me to accept the universe as unknowable as the unconscious is, in the same breath, the same sentence, the same text, the same book, the same library, the same conversation

¶ Babel is, I'd want to say, the normal state of affairs. It is not a kind of mythological metaphor we have outlived, bypassed, succeeded or forgotten. We are Babel, this talk is Babelan, our ability to listen is Babelian, the words we use are Babelic, the babble we utter is Babelistic, the responses we have to it are Babelasceous, the arguments we counter it with are Babelositous, our inabilities to understand across other languages are Babelous. The house of the murmur of language is the house of Babel, where all sayings in all languages both have and find their home

¶ how then does my small personal library sit alongside or inside Babel, which is no longer a tower or any vertical, penile structure, but a kind of ground-cover, like a moss that slithers over the surface of the earth, that creeps out and obscures the soil in which it grows. The prospect that there is life outside Babel, outside the library, is a question I have yet to ask

5

The limits of the book as object

¶ haunted by the life, death, and erotics of the body of the book, I am unable to utter any statement of the form 'I love books' or 'I love reading'. Could such love be narcissistic, the book touched by a reader who in turn wants to be touched by the book. But the book as object and whisperer in your ear is a false object of desire and in turn, turning it over in the mind, in the hands, on the bed of the press, the book itself as an object objects

'Warning : *The Telephone Book* is going to resist you' is one of the opening sentences I admire most, in its resistance to my most patient endeavours. Here, all the *eros* and *thanatos* one could wish for is laid out, testing one's skill and desire to bring it forth to life, again and again. The telephone, writes Avital Ronell, who delivered the above warning, has no off switch. To the technological, she purrs, there are only modes of being switched on, the technological 'does not disappear but goes into remission', a condition for which there is no cure, only modes of being on hold is there, similarly, no such animal as the closed book, that it too, already open before we are, does not close when we ourselves are shut down. If we, as human prostheses of the technological, are always switched on, then our awareness of being always available to the call of the telephone, to the opening of the book, is not to be presumed

¶ shortly before the first conference on the history of the book in New Zealand was held in 1995, I was privileged, in conversation with D F McKenzie, to share a mutual distaste for the term 'print culture'. We both thought then that the field of our different activities was more accurately 'the book, loosely understood', which permitted attention to be paid to newspapers, magazines, digests, broadsides, broadsheets, diaries, account books, proclamations, pamphlets, acts of parliament and so on, along with whatever documentary materials accompany them. We also speculated whether the term 'print culture' would or could ever have the full range of its implications played out in the academic realm

each day, each of us undertakes a range of readings on a variety of material substrates not usually considered under the heading of 'the book, loosely understood'. Even a short list of them would include : watches, clocks, calendars, invoices, street signs, price tags, bus and train tickets, dance cards, flour bags, menus, noticeboards, credit cards, coinage, junk mail, directional and exit signs, bank notes, billboards, business cards, theatre tickets, shop signs, letterboxes, vehicle number plates, gravestones, fashion labels, product packaging, metal plaques, identity cards, receipts for payment, etc. All are modes of textual transmission locatable as 'print culture' but not as 'the book, loosely understood'. Put another way, all books are modes of textual transmission, but not all modes of textual transmission are books. For the most part, these small, fast, apparently ephemeral acts of reading are barely registered by us *as* acts of reading

it suggests that for many of us, the term 'reading' is reserved for a select number of what I am calling 'modes of textual transmission' rather than for the totality of reading acts of any kind whatever. Or, it may suggest that we have gotten into a habit of calling 'reading' only those acts of reading that for any of us are particularly affective or important or meaningful or 'cultural' (taken in a higher or simply different sense than culture as 'the totality of what a people does'). But if the book now takes its place under 'print culture', it lines up with all other modes of textual transmission as one mode among others as the book 'tightly understood', the book as an object alongside the gravestone, bus ticket, street sign, magazine, e-book, and so on. If for some this appears to devalue the book, take the edge off its privileged status, for me it frees the book to shine more brightly within the array of textual transmitters that form a significant part of our environment. What binds the objects of print culture together is not any possible notion of 'the book', but the totality of all written and printed artefacts, whatever their technologies. When notions of 'reading' attach only to specific kinds of reading, then all other kinds are left unaccounted for. Perhaps it is time to reintegrate all acts of reading and all modes of textual transmission and all types of script and print into a larger notion of literacy

⁋ in W W Skeat's *Etymological Dictionary of the English Language* (1st edition 1879-1882), he gives for the word 'book' a nicely doubled and troubling definition : 'a volume; a written composition'. The difference between a physical book and any text it may contain is well understood and is as clearly exhibited in the mass-market paperback as it is in the e-book. But when we talk and write about the book, we often slide from one of Skeat's apparitional binaries to the other without acknowledging the shift. Thruout the western media 'book review' almost invariably means 'text review', and matters pertaining to the book as a codex are usually referred to as matters of aesthetic presentation rather than bearers of historical information. Skeat's written composition is the topic of discussion whereas the volume is almost never the topic of discussion. The public book review is not the site for the sort of complex readings indicated by D F McKenzie's 'the book itself is an expressive means'

Skeat's binaries are usually taken as either/or options, one focuses on one at the expense of the other, but I am adopting them as the whole caboodle, the whole definition of a book as an object, a volume *and* a written composition, codex+text = book as object. For somehow we still have to account for the simplicity that books as here defined are still manufactured in their millions every day, across most of the planet, in their old, fixed, stubborn, familiar, conservative and instantly recognisable form, a form that needs neither analysis nor investigation for the object to be identified as a book. When did we ever get it wrong

¶ the limits of the book as an object are easily identified as its front and back covers, with or without a spine. Within that perimeter any word(s) and any image(s) can appear. Beatrice Warde's model of the goblet and the wine springs, at least to my mind. Into that goblet the finest vintage or any old *vino collapso* can be poured, and at least from a logical point of view any text can appear in any specific codex. Most general readers treat texts as if they could be conveyed by any number of different media, where the medium does not qualify the meaning of the text, suggesting a disembodied, disembedded act of reading in which the particular mode of transmission might only be a matter of personal preference. Indeed, some enthusiasts for the computer *contra* the codex have triumphantly argued that the text has at last been set free from its carrier, the message from its medium, in an old-fashioned mechanism of politics and commerce known as 'divide and rule'. Even so, the seeds for this separation have been sown in the writings of some of the very people who have valued above all else the roles of the codex and of printing in the interactive multiple language context of the ongoing process of cultural life. Warde's famous line, 'printing should be invisible', treats the carriers of texts as matters of appropriate presentation rather than sites of historical, textual, and contextual information yet, the separation of text and vehicle remains an issue, even in the language used to characterise it. A recent conference paper cheerfully referred to this desirable liberation of the text from its medium as an 'amputation'. But amputation disfigures, maims, and disables. McKenzie's note that 'every book tells a story quite apart from that recounted by its text' acknowledges that the codex and its text are amenable to

separate readings. But 'amputation' is designed to disallow and disavow the readability of the technologies, hard and soft, of the electronic vehicle. All we are supposed to get is the text and nothing but the text. But the notion that these technologies should be invisible, after all they are material commodities and do not live in cyberspace, is as unacceptable a proposition as that printing should be invisible. We are perfectly capable of seeing what is in front of us and understanding how it got there without being exhorted, against the material evidence, to perceive only the text and never the vehicle of its conveyance

¶ when defining the book as an object, tightly understood, as codex+text, the field of attention is narrowed down as the book takes its place among a collection of textual transmitters (whether 'vehicular' or 'interactive', in the terms of Jerome McGann) that includes all the substrates of print culture and all the products of computer technology. It only confuses matters to use 'book' as both the name of an instance of print culture and as the general category of the products of print culture as a whole. Some commentators would have us redefine 'book' to accommodate new means for the presentation of texts, but I cannot see how this can be clarifying in current context. Do not, instead, the new means of text conveyance allow us, require us, to redefine the book to more usefully distinguish the book from them. The products of computer technology never come on to the market without a name, whether 'computer', 'iPod' or 'e-book'. Why label them 'book' as well. As objects, as products, they are as distinguishable from books as telephones are from tv sets

a related claim made by some that the codex-style book is a product whereas the electronic 'book' is a service is disingenuous. The profits to be made on the sale of the hardware are considerable, and if you don't buy the hardware you cannot read the electronic texts. Such commentators, in thrall to the supersession fallacy, want to discredit the codex as a legitimate factor in the new world of so-called 'democratic' and 'egalitarian' access to world knowledge. If they had their way, all texts would be located in the hands of a single service provider, Google for instance, instead of an array of book and other publishers, each exhibiting different values & considerations when it comes to reflecting the multiplicity of human possibilities. As if what they wanted was the abolition of intellectual and cultural biodiversity in the otherwise messy networks of textual origination. The words lurking behind this electronic push, but not used as they might alert us to the real issue, are 'technotopia' and the 'singularity', two of the ugliest possibilities in the whole field of electronic communications. The 'choice' offered in this democratic dream is singular, or no choice: if one wants to know something,

the one place one may go to is Google, and Google has had
recently to be taken to court in order for them to even register that their absorption of other people's texts into their
control constitutes theft of intellectual property on a grand
scale. I do not deny the unprecedented and extraordinary
access we have now to a vast network of information, nor the
value to us all of the resources that the computer has opened
up for researcher, reader, scholar & dilettante alike. The
danger is not in the computer per se, but in the ownership
of the portal to those resources. One portal = a monopoly
everyone should be concerned about. Multiple portals is no
doubt the proper corrective

¶ for most scholars nowadays, only a specialised and close
reading of the codex-and-the-text-within-it will ensure that
the text remains at least in some measure embedded and
embodied within the book or whatever structure that per-
mits us to engage with the text in the first place. Literary
critics, textual critics and bibliographers have become well
used in recent decades to reading both the codex and its text
in ways that allow interactive connections to become visible
and operative between the two. Even the standard mass-market paperback is available for the double analysis that McGann
has elaborated as a back and forth focus between linguis-
tic codes and bibliographical codes. But there is another and
growing body of people who are taking the scholars' terms
of analysis of finished books and utilising them as a broad
intellectual basis for the manufacture of new books, as if mir-
roring Igor Stravinsky on music, as 'the poetics of work yet to

be done'. This growing body of people are the makers of artist's books

the artist's book seeks to take that specialised close reading of the codex-and-text-together as its ordinary, everyday, basic mode of readerly engagement. Taking it, as the bibliographer and textual scholar do, that the book and the text are to be read as a simultaneous and unitary whole, the artist's book maker begins with this notion as a conceptual factor in the very making of the book itself. Here for instance is a definition by archivist, commentator, and artist's book seller, Ulises Carrión: 'Bookworks are books that are conceived as an expressive unity, that is to say, where the message is the sum of all materials and formal elements'. To quote McKenzie again, 'every book tells a story quite apart from that recounted by its text'

complicating the discussion on artist's books for bookish people is that the critical discourse that has accompanied the rise of the artist's book is predominantly art and art history discourse rather than book and book history discourse. While there is some overlap between these discourses, there is a fair amount of anecdotal evidence for the view that the artist's book has replaced the fine press book in the budgets of many institutional buyers in the United States and Australia. In Australia, it is hard to prevent fine press books from being referred to as artist's books, and the term artist's book is being increasingly co-opted by press edition makers for the results of their labour, because institutions everywhere have given the artist's book a cultural and intellectual status higher than that of the press book. We are not always or simply looking at complexities of definition

the pressure however to redefine the book comes as much from the field of the artist's book as it does from the computer industry, and as far as I can see, the pressures from both sides have failed to come up with an appropriate and usable definition. Part of the problem stems from the view that the book should be redefined according to the increasingly multiple uses or purposes the 'new' book is given to serve. But I have yet to see any such purpose articulated that is not already served by the traditional codex, particularly along the lines of the merging of text and image. For the most part artist's book makers work within the structure of the codex for their work, tho some have on occasion abandoned the codex altogether for a three-dimensional structure with multiple surfaces and text &/or images on those surfaces. Having done that, why would anyone want to use the word 'book' instead of 'sculpture' for the thing made. When the computer industry or artist's book makers (those who abandon the codex as a structure) co-opt the term 'book' for what they make and wish to sell, they often do so by stretching the definition of 'book' so substantially as to violate our everyday knowledge that a book is a codex plus text/image. No one should have any objection to new technologies being developed as novel modes of textual or cultural transmission, nor to the growth of a field of artistic endeavour in which three-dimensional, sculptural works of art are made with multiple surfaces, some of which may bear texts and images. But a book is an object before it can be a concept or a metaphor, and once those concepts or metaphors leave the literal object behind, other names for the results are in order

¶ when it comes to looking at the limits of the book as an object, it remains hard if not impossible not to see those limits as the front and back covers of a codex+text. This applies 103 as well to the paperback, the fine press book and the artist's book. The relation that the book tightly understood has to the focus of bibliographical study, the book loosely understood (i.e. print culture), is one that opens the possibility, beyond the book as object, to the book as a concept or metaphor. To quote from the Call for Papers for a recent BSANZ conference on The Limits of the Book : 'Although the sequentially-read codex has been the normative form of the book for many centuries, alternative physical forms ranging from the scroll to a box of randomly ordered sheets, to a dossier of facsimile documents, to an electronic tablet *challenge and extend the category of object we call 'book'.*' (my italics) What if one replaced the italicised end of this sentence with 'require us to clarify and consolidate the category of object we call 'book'.' The original passage relies on the assumption that 'book' can usefully serve as the generalised name of the cluster of all modes of textual transmission and the name of one of those modes at the same time. The replacement passage allows all modes of textual transmission to line up alongside the book as codex+text, each with its own mode of operation, its own set of social practices, and its own name

¶ one of the problems that nestle inside the notion of the book
has to do with the no longer universally accepted notion of
the divine origins of the primary texts of the so-called 'book
religions'. The book written or dictated or divinely inspired
by a monotheistic god bestowed a sovereign status on the
book, the tribal memory of which seems to remain with many
of us, even those for whom the god is not operative and the
book is not singular. Canadian writer Anne Carson tells of
writing stories when a small child, and being chided by her
father on the grounds that there are enough stories in the
Old Testament for anyone to know. The poet and anthologist
Jerome Rothenberg believes in a kind of 'primal book', which
lies behind all other books, and of which each book is merely an infinitesimal earthly portion of the primal infinite text.
Many secular people still have this residual sense that there
is a primary Book which makes all worldly books possible.
It's hard for me to escape the feeling that something like this
resides behind the computer industry's dystopic vision that all
texts should have a single 'home', a single site of availability,
as if cyberspace were to become the computer-based equiva-
lent of the ancient library of Alexandria, which was intended
to house all the books of the world

¶ I wonder if there is a kind of parallelogram functioning
here. In line with Newton's third law of motion, that for any
action there is an equal and opposite reaction, western scholarship's reading of the carriers of texts emerged coincident
with the computer beginning to assume part of the responsibility for making texts available to more and more people

more quickly than before, and with a diminished capacity for reading history in the carrier. At the same time, is the recently renewed assault on the codex by the computer industry paralleled by the recently increased attention to the intense materiality of the artist's book. Without proposing equality of reaction or one to one causation, it seems to me that all four aspects are simultaneously part of the huge change taking place in the sphere of interconnected communications world- wide. The Arts and Crafts movement of the late nineteenth century was a response to the mechanisation of manufacturing processes that provided the society with the material objects of daily life : pottery, glass blowing, furniture making, weaving, lace-making, printing, and binding among others. Such technologies rendered obsolete by industrialisation were released from having social and commercial purposes into the hands of individuals for personal and creative purposes. In terms of print technology, the change enabled the development of 'fine printing', from the 'little typographical experiment' of William Morris to the present day. At that time, the commercial book was not under threat as the primary vehicle for the transmission of texts at the highest and lowest intellectual and cultural levels. Now that the codex is under articulated threat by business interests (even tho many otherwise sensible people are taking the threat seriously) the artist's book emerges in the face of a proposed dematerialisation of 'the book'. At stake perhaps is the revelation/obfuscation of historical process. In the same way that the typographical operations performable on the computer obscure the histories that made those options available, the availability of texts via the internet obscures the histories that made the texts accessible to the computer in the first place. It has even been suggested that the privilege of writing itself should be removed from the individual and given over to the community, a 'true' democracy of composition, and that the computer should be the site of writing instead of the notebook or manuscript, leading to the obliteration of handwriting (one of the individual's most sovereign signatures) and the universal dissemination of the keyboard as the site of writing, the site of literacy itself. Personally, I think the book as codex+text will prevail, not because left to its own devices it will somehow defeat the computer in the long run, but because, in taking the book as codex+text, we can now re-examine the book as an object and reintegrate it into our already growing but everyday understanding of the altered situation in which textual transmission in general is being transformed by the increasingly sophisticated capacities of the computer. In my view, only by recreating the book as an object, as a codex+text, can that re-examination be usefully conducted

6

Exergue : destroying the books

¶ this is not about libricide, or the cultural genocide that attempts to obliterate a culture & its people by eradicating their documents, but the destruction of books by makers, owners, publishers, libraries, galleries, readers, in fact anyone who takes a book and throws it out, or destroys it by burning it or consigning it to the trash. In this case, the destroyer is likely to be friendly to the object, and the motives are likely to be economic ones or matters of convenience & house-keeping, bad management or stupidity

¶ destroying books & other documents is part of the normal business of daily life, of which the genocidal kind is a complex special case — an elaboration of an already active everyday process of cleaning up, however that is understood in particular circumstances, personal or institutional

¶ is destroying books different in any fundamental way from destroying anything else. The heirlooms, dinner plates, knick-knacks, furniture, typewriters, linen, frying pans etc of parents & grandparents, how do we feel about throwing them out, and is it different from throwing out their old books which, right or wrong, it may be thought no one would now want to read. Is the genocidal impulse simply that, among the things that can be destroyed, books are specially suited to the purpose, as is the destruction of churches, synagogues, mosques, schools, universities, palaces and the infrastructures of power generation, military bases, water catchments, transport centers and so on. On another hand, non-genocidal destruction continues apace, of forests, buildings, farmland, waterways etc in the name of progress or business or whatever other rationale is dreamt up, even if pockets of resistance remain operative

¶ there's no census on how many books, newspapers, pamphlets, magazines etc are destroyed on a daily basis all over the planet. One could point to the vast amount of paper recycling in major cities — every second week across Melbourne tonnes of paper in the form of newspapers, books & magazines are collected from homes and recycled mainly for cardboard & product packaging. In this sense, destroying books is regarded as an environmental benefit. But that the materials are of recent origin, yesterday's newspaper, last year's telephone book, flyers for local tradespeople etc, does not mean that documents and documentation are not being destroyed. What is destroyed by recycling. At a conference in 2007 an illustrated talk was given showing that the history of apple-box and other fruit box labels in a particular region could tell a story about history in technological, economic and sociological terms. What's true of apple-box labels could thus be true of any & every sort of labelling & packaging. There are individuals who collect early product packaging, biscuit tins & boxes, flour bags, jam jars, cartons that once contained any number of products bought from grocery stores, hardware shops etc. Some of these people have acquired considerable knowledge along the way of their collecting which, in most cases, will die with them. And when an unsympathetic family is cleaning up their estates, what then, where will the collection go. Books after all can be seen as just another item under the heading of printed clutter in contexts like these, and the question whether to keep or throw out has to be made

¶ over the years I have bought and sold many books. A few books, acquired for purposes not to do with my own reading interests, have been tossed into the recycling bin because I had no interest in either keeping them or seeing that they reached other hands. In these cases the issue was more to do with my view of the authors than with my view of the objects being books per se

¶ pulping unsold or slow-selling books is part of the normal business of publishing in the west. Done at the end of the fiscal year it's to reap the benefits of depreciation for tax purposes. Publishers have given authors various reasons other than depreciation for pulping their books — "the distributor needs the shelf space" and "we printed more copies than originally intended" are two I know about — but the effect is the same : the author's royalties are reduced, and the book becomes potentially (it's not guaranteed) more valuable to the second-hand book trade. Some publishers inform authors about the pulping of their books before the event, giving the author the option of taking delivery of the unsold copies, and some publishers inform authors after the event when the books have already been pulped. It is rare that a whole edition is pulped by a publisher, but it has happened where legal issues or topical ones have overtaken the imminent publication and made it redundant

¶ the public library and the university library have this extraordinary capacity : they make a single volume available to a large number of people, whether by lending or by being able to be referenced. But books that sit on a shelf for a long time without being used risk being de-accessioned. De-accessioning is a standard procedure among both types of library. There are two modes of de-accessioning (whatever the reasons given) : destroying the book, and selling it. The former means no one gets that volume any more, and the latter means just one person does. But some would see that there is a world of value-difference between the two modes, even tho a single volume's demise may not affect the continued availability of that edition at other venues

¶ the library is not necessarily a final destination for a book. Some books are circulated internally within the building, others outside. The latter is usually temporary, but sometimes permanent, and this has always been the library's nature. Books leave my library by being sold, by being taken on temporary journeys, by being recycled. Whatever pangs I have had at books leaving me, they have often been due to an unwanted loss, and usually because of financial difficulty. I find within me no trace of any sense that a book, as an object, has an absolute or 'sacred' value

¶ it is not uncommon that a family or family member will seek to maintain a collection of books, documents, diaries or letters by gifting the collection to a library. If accepted, the collection then has to be catalogued & shelved, and for this there are costs to be drawn from budgets already more or less committed. For the library's purposes these volumes might be better dispersed among the rest of the collection, in subject areas where the volumes are more likely to be identified by readers for use. But this may be against the wishes of the family, which may believe that the collection has a value beyond the sum of its separable parts, and it is this value they wish to preserve. Then, some librarians do not necessarily feel bound by arrangements made by their predecessors. And any number of reasons can be found to either move books from shelves to storage or from storage to pulp. Most of us don't get to know about these processes when they occur, but they occur more commonly than we know

¶ is there a difference between destroying books per se, and destroying a particular book whether a volume or an edition. For who values what. An atheist may not at all be concerned if every Gideon bible went up in smoke. A religious may not at all be concerned if every secular book went up in smoke. But this is not really what I'm getting at, tho it is interesting to see how deeply the notion of the book as a sacred object is embedded in our talk about destroying books. To shrug off the beliefs of millions is no light matter, and may include pulping impulses of one's own

¶ what is gained by the publication of a book that any of us personally will never want to read. What is lost by the disappearance of a book that any of us will never want to read

¶ *Author Offers Rebate for Destroying Competitor's Books*
Torn Covers to Provide Proof

this is a genuine lift off a blog. While the commercial and ideological imperatives are clear, the author invites readers to destroy books of his 'choosing', books not written by him but already in the field, as a hook to getting a discount on his. Presumably another author may offer the same bargain for the destruction of the first offer. And poets & novelists, historians & biographers, crime writers & romance novelists could do the same. . . a whole new layer of competition in the book trade. One could even name the particular authors whose works one would like to see shredded. . . ah, they float before me now. . .

¶ at a writer's festival (in Melbourne, yesterday) an artist sits at a table with a box and a leather purse of medical & surgical instruments & needles, cutting up the covers & pages of a book, rendering the reading purpose of the book inoperative but making a small & elegant sculpture in the name of art. He is enjoying himself, people are courteous & interested in what he is doing, it is something he has done for over a decade, his work is meticulous, with the kind of care one expects from a fine craftsman, but each moment is fraught with an anxiety in which he half-expects someone to approach him in outrage &/or distress that he is violating a sacred object. But what interests me about this event is that no writers among the hundreds present at the festival seem to be interested in the work of the artist or in the transformation of the book into art taking place in their midst

¶ in the interests of secularising the book, any sense of its 'sacredness' or 'aura' has to be dispelled. Only this would allow one to destroy a book or document without having to believe something like a human issue is at stake. My life is in books. Books are not sacred objects to me tho I take good care of them. Every creature dies. Every thing disintegrates. How to honor that, yet deal with the human capacity or interest in conserving what it values, like an heirloom, a cultural arte-fact, a socially significant object or document, or a book

¶ it's clear that, whatever anyone's personal attitude or response to destroying books is, libraries and publishers have long ceased to treat books as sacred objects. If 'sacred' is not an appropriate term to use of books per se, then what term is or, why does the term 'sacred' need to be replaced at all, what is lost by letting the term simply fall out of use. A book, after all, is a thing, like any other thing, one of the ten thousand things, but a thing nonetheless that one can choose to value among all the things that, as it were, compete for value in a product-littered world

¶ as if there were a kind of gap or hesitation between the secularity of a book and the value anyone places on it. All books are things, but not all things are culturally neutral, and no books are sacred, ergo a space opens up for words appropriate for the gap. What shall they be, what sort of gloss do we lay over the book

¶ one could ask, what is the point of a book, what, in other words, does it point to. If a book is a thing in itself, a thing for itself, it is not a thing by itself, for it sits, there, alongside all the other books, alongside us

¶ it is perfectly possible to see that terms like 'sacred' and 'aura' are not interchangeable, and one doesn't deal with the problem of how to register what is 'special' about a poem or a painting by replacing one word with the other. Walter Benjamin's term 'aura' is specific to an original work, aspects of which 'wither' under the processes of reproduction. But these aspects are not invisible, not some kind of felt presence independent of the physical detail of the work itself. Benjamin's 'aura' is something like the totality of the physical details in all their complexity, details which distinguish the work from any reproduced copy. The term 'sacred' does not work this way — in some societies a stick selected from the bush can be invested with sanctity for the limited time of a particular ritual, after which the sacred object becomes a stick again and returned to the bush. The sacred is thus an investment in an object or story and is not concerned with the details of a work's making. A Michelangelo or Leonardo or Giotto painting can point to the sacred, but is not sacred of itself

¶ but many talk/write as if 'sacred' and 'aura' are interchangeable, nevertheless. What is happening here. Is 'aura' a kind of secular investment, where something like religion is given away but a religious 'sense' is retained. If this is so, is what is 'retained' inherent in the work or in the engagement with it. If aura is inherent in the work, why is it there and not in every possible object whatever. And is it the case that the aura of engagement can only occur with a work of art and not anything else. I am able happily to accept Benjamin's notion of the aura as it refers to original works, but its use as a kind of non-religious parallel to the sacred is another, and different, matter

¶ is it not rather the case that the question of aura emerges every time a human pays very close attention to any phenomenon whatsoever : a work of art, a person, a flower, an animal, a river, a mountain, a line of words, a string of terns, anything that is, that we turn to (always a question of re-focusing the gaze). Attending to a work of art is thus no more or less than a specific instance of a wider pattern of human behaviour. The artwork is not special because of some characteristic of itself, but because it is a recognisable participant in a range of human behaviour based on a range of agreements about value

¶ when it comes to the book, what if the purpose of a book, after all, and after all the history of the book, is to return us to nothing more or less than the conversation that the book authorised away from talk, so that we might talk again, more richly than before. The purpose of the book in this sense is to continue, even perpetuate, our conversation, in other words, our orality

¶ could it be that the twentieth century engagement with the text will prove to be a wrong turning, an anomaly, that speech is indeed primary for humans, that text is in the service of speech and not the other way around. Or maybe that the relation of speech/text is more properly or usefully the to & fro of movement between them and not any primacy of one term over the other. All humans talk before we read, and we read parental body language before we read text. No talk happens without an accompanying language of the body. Oral culture is body-talk, not mouth-talk alone

¶ books have not replaced orality, but have added to orality's store of possibility. With each new book we have something else to talk about as well as write about. With each new television program the same. Television simulates, for the most part, body-talk, an oral rather than a visual medium, will it never shut up

¶ when human partnerships break down, relations with once cherished objects, like books, can change dramatically. People have destroyed books and other objects that were previously a valued part of the relationship, a displacement perhaps, instead of destroying the person

¶ the value here is not 'sacred', a 'place apart', but a place incorporate, a place internalised, not transcendental but immanent, a function of an inner life, like a digested text that one wishes to disgorge or cut out, as one might attack in rage a once-loved book with a knife

¶ if one once loved a book's content, then later found it offended one, how could that content be eliminated from the reader's body

¶ even Edmond Jabès, taking it, or so it seems, that the word 'god' stands not for an existent being, but for the absence of that being, kept using the word, and the word for an official of its religion, 'rabbi', so often it seems more like an obsession than a rejection. As if, in attempting to eject the words from his body, they got stuck in his throat

¶ as if, in burning the books, their ashes swirled in the wind and attached themselves to one, or even entered one's open mouth so one never stopped choking on them

¶ once in the system, always in, is that it. Destroying the books = destroying the self, is that it. Or, may not be expunged, but may be transformed, is that it

¶ there is no census of the number of writings that will never find a publisher, will never be made book

❡ we think of the destruction of books as an event coming after publication, but how is that different from preventing writings from being published. For many, the idea of destroying books is intimately bound up with censorship, and censorship can certainly take place at the point of agreeing or not agreeing to publish. What we have then is a sea of writings, all in process of breaking their news on shore, but only some of them will remain on land, the rest subsiding again into the sea of publishable possibility. Some of those that reach land and do get published will then be pulped or burned or recycled. If 'destruction' is not the best term for the silencing of writings before publication, then what is the word for 'all writings for which publication is either denied at the point of publication or after that point'. If there were such a term, might it bypass the negative visceral feelings many experience on learning of the destruction of books. A book may come to being or cease to be as any plant or flower may flourish or perish

❡ how might we separate our response to the genocidal destruction of books from our response to the everyday destruction of books, and both from the failure of writings to reach publication at all

❡ *modalities of retrieval* : in spite of everything, the matter is complicated by acts of retrieval. Even publishers will attempt to keep a book in circulation by way of remaindering. Authors will buy up remainders or accept delivery of books planned for pulping. Some books have been literally retrieved from rubbish bins and given to others, including their authors. Some of those books have been bought & reworked for republishing in altered form. Out-of-print or rare texts are regularly put on the web, free or at a cost. Some publishers are making their back-lists available as PDF files in order to keep the publisher as current agency as much as gaining continued currency for their out-of-print titles. The recent 'print-on-demand' capability allows increasing numbers of individuals to publish books of their own writing. And scholarship everywhere, by examining historical works no longer in circulation, is constantly making knowledge of otherwise unread or unremarked texts available to others. Many of these acts of retrieval, even to the point of conservation, are performed by the same agencies & institutions that perform acts of destruction

¶ no text can escape a critical reading.
   no text can claim absolute acceptance.
   all texts are modified, altered, qualified, accepted and
      rejected by other texts.
   all texts are members of or participants in the totality of texts.
   new texts are appearing to reading every day.
   some texts are disappearing from reading every day.
   the process of textual generation and dispersal and disap-
      pearance is continuous.
   the destruction of texts, is part of the generation and shap-
      ing of the life of text in the human community.
   the coming & going of texts is part of the dynamic life of
      text, and the normal state of affairs.
   one can never look into the same text twice

Endnote : the books to come

Today, the project of future understanding remains the fiction that it always will have been, an insight that can be neither proven nor verified. Still, this fiction, generated out of the exigencies of an inescapable temporality, is understanding's truth.

— *Avital Ronell* [Stupidity, p157]

the endnote is without end. With each new book
the multiplication continues. Often I read them first.
The endnote as the first word of the book. An inexplicit
incipit. This is the opening and closing gambit
all in one, in the opening and closing of the reading
eye. Without them where would you be, back at the
beginning, which had never begun
and will never end

naming is exact & inexact

when Jacques Derrida, Maurice Blanchot and Edmond Jabès
write about 'the book', what they seem to have in mind is not
an object, but a text. Their writings are not informed by twen-
tieth-century developments in textual criticism, art history, or
the artist's book

Very early, writing was recognised as a means to spread legal orders
and otherwise communicate a spoken word. From the beginning, the
main purpose of writing was to record the voice of the speaker — in
other words, the writing systems were oral. . . . Oral writing systems
are the concrete reality behind the term "the voice of authority". . . .
Oral writing systems are voice-based (phonetic-based) and inclusive;
they record speech along with semantic sense. Modern writing systems
are sense-based (semantic-based) and exclusive, except for the infor-
mational content, they convey little information to the reader. . . .
Semantic-based writing systems are rooted in data transmission; their
primary purpose is to convey information. Phonetic-based writing
systems are rooted in oral communication; their primary purpose is to
convey a record of a "text" as spoken — with all those factors that serve
to identify that specific text as itself and no other (an entity).

— Rochelle Altman, Absent voices [p. 1-4]

this is a step further than saying prose is paraphrasable and poetry is not. One can also put alongside it that the poetry reading as a structural component of contemporary literature is flourishing. The web and internet not only make written texts more widely and quickly available but web videos, YouTube and blogs are making the reading by the poet more and more familiar. In New York hardly a day goes by when it's not possible to attend a poetry reading somewhere in the city, and some account is needed as to why 'the voice of the poet, the voice of the author' is a requirement at poetry book launches — a recognition perhaps that the semantic text, or even the text alone, is not enough, that there is a need to re-humanize texts from which the author as agent has been drained for far too long. It suits, does it not, totalizing structures for individuals to accept their relative insignificance in the determination of social & cultural value. But time & again poets are told at readings that poems that have been read somewhat stolidly on the page have suddenly 'come alive' thru being read aloud by the poet, and that the hearer will now go back to the poems on the page for a more lively reading, which is also, now, a hearing. Poetry, then, as a phonetic-based, oral writing system, designed to convey the voice of the speaker conveying speech. Sounds good to me

among : the basic relation of everything to everything
the multiple foci of every one highlights
every thing now & then here & there

124

what I am now vividly aware of is that very early in my life I
decided against all forms of political action — an array of
power structures I wished to avoid, and an insight that I would
be no less petty or misguided or uninformed or narrow-mind-
ed than anyone else, properties that consensus or majority
vote were powerless to change, not even by mass protests,
mass killing

what will be my books
          to come
     powerless to effect social life or change
          not to speak out
     but, to speak   the magpie lands
          on the fence   twenty turtledoves
     whoosh off the grass   which one
          am I

I want 'the book' to be no more of a metaphor than, say, 'the chair' — 'the chair' is a concept that denotes a class of objects, saying nothing about the relative value of any particular chair in relation to any other chair. 'The book' is a concept that denotes a class of objects (codex+text), saying nothing about the relative value of any particular book in relation to any other book. Unless we can deal with 'the book' on this basic level, we risk all sorts of difficulties when it comes to being precise about specific instances

look at any book, however made
assume you have no label for it,
what are you looking at, what words
could you use, words that are
non-definitional, non-interpretive
words that assume and do not assume
that you are looking, simply, at
a work of art, where what you say
is structured by what you see
and not by prior discussion based on
concepts drawn from activities
from which the work diverges
or intentions which the complexity of
the work efficiently conceal, without
in other words, the label, however
lengthy, however complex, however
insisted upon by the anxiety of the
artist who wishes, against all wisdom
of the ages, to be understood

however the book survives
its contours
literal physical form and mode
of use
the logic you could say
of what separates the book
from any other thing
will remain & remind
maculate as the bird scrapping
over food
secure in the ample
recognition of itself
the book
codex+text
whatever co-option or metaphor
is used to obscure
the inevitable uses & misuses
that will be made
of it

since D F McKenzie wrote 'The book itself is an expressive means', this proposition has been repeated and elaborated many times by many people in many contexts. The view however is often used to reject or dismiss notions of 'form and content', sometimes taken as an either/or binary in which the terms are used as if they were mutually exclusive, as if those who did find the terms useful were hoodwinked into believing that what can be said about one cannot be said about the other. In discussing the normal trade paperback, it's obvious that a single form can be employed to contain an incredible range of content, that the codex is a more or less fixed form into which multiple and conflicting contents can be poured. But McKenzie and many others have long shown that even a blank book 'contains history', that a wordless codex (the fixed form) will already be loaded with content without being marked by writing, printing, or image-making of any kind form & content can be shown to exist in spaces than can be close enough to overlap, or distant enough not to. There seems in current book art to be a dream of finding a way of 'making book' in which there is no separation of form & content, that the book made is a singular event, in which notions of form & content dissolve into a single phenomenon or dissipate so that a different modality of discussion can emerge out of the engagement with the unique new-made 'book'. In my own fine book making, for instance, the notions of form & content are practically non-operative as I enter the printery each day to get on with the work. I have the materials and I have the marks to be made and I work in a single frame of mind & heart as the day requires. But once a book is made, any book, any kind of book, trade book or fine book or artist's book, discussion can roam around the object as a single phenomenon all we wish, but we are still going to say things about its shape & structure that cannot be said about its markings. In other words, form & content are more useful modes of talking about a book after the event of its making, not before. The trouble with the terms 'form' & 'content' is that the word 'form' masks the simplicity that form is already saturated with content, but the value of the terms is that they permit us to maintain the principle of indeterminacy: one cannot talk about structure and markings at the same time: one cannot look at a text and thru a text at the same time: one cannot focus on manufacture & meaning at the same time — each requires a shift, however minute, however fast, between one and the other and back again. One cannot measure, says the indeterminacy principle, the location and the velocity of an object in space at the same time. It's the same with the book it seems to me, and the terms form & content are therefore better seen and used as relative & operational terms and not as absolute & ontological ones. Whatever the case, and whatever one's intentions, they are still useful terms in the discussion about the book, and the principle of indeterminacy still pertains whether we wish it to or not. And it is the fate of all new structures, that have developed or emerged out of the artist's engagement with the energies of making, that those structures can be used by others as forms into which to pour new content, and all trade books, fine books, and artists books have this potential independent of their makers' intentions

thought may as validly outstrip one's practice
as practice may outstrip one's thought

praxis is not to be presumed (i.e. practice based
on an established form or theory (tho Klein has it
as 'the opposite of theory'; doing, exercise, business

even 'practice' has the sense of repetition, following
a form (as the practice of music, accounting,
medicine, or printing (one is, as they say,
a practitioner

'. . . que tout, au monde, existe pour aboutir a un livre'
Mallarmé

'. . . everything in the world exists in order to end up as a book'
Mallarmé, trans Michael Gibbs

'. . . everything in the world exists to result in a book'
Mallarmé, trans Svetlana Boym

'. . . everything in the world exists to end up as a book'
Mallarmé, trans Barbara Johnson

You are right. Mallarmé wrote that the world is made to end
up AS a book...'aboutir a un livre' can also mean to lead to in a
sense (like our 'abut') but it never meant 'to end up IN a book'.
Marion May Campbell (personal communication

try this : everything exists in the world to lead [one?] to a book

& this : every book exists to lead [one?] to a thing in the world

in each case, a book, not 'the' book

what is the book to which any individual & given thing in the world
    might lead me
what are the things in the world that lead me to any
    individual & given book
                                books that are
                                books to come

no thing & no book
is exempt from this
possibility

Mallarmé wrote his essays 'about the book' from his vantage as a writer, as many of us do. His famous sentence is very attractive to many of us because it directs attention a priori to the book. But what if I were a carpenter, what could I say then. What is it that any individual & given thing might lead us to. A building? where almost anything in the world, given an accommodating scale, could live inside a house or building. Even plants & animals could be housed there. Everything in the world exists in order to end up as a house. For a gardener, everything in the world might exist to end up as a garden. But then a house or a garden may exist in order to end up as, or lead to, a book. Yet a priority of the book bothers me as much as does a priority of the text

    every book in the world
        exists
  in order to end up
      be in
  or lead to
      the world

    the book as
      a worldly thing
  not the world as
      a bookish thing

    the relation is not
      symmetrical

the logical unidimensional relation between books, scrolls, tablets, e-books and the world is that the world came first, long before human life, longer before language, longer before the marks of writing, and longer still before books, scrolls, tablets, e-books etc were invented. Any view which denies or ignores this unidimensional hierarchy has some explaining to do

The Book : What did Mallarmé mean by this word?

On the face of it, a fairly innocuous question. It comes from Maurice Blanchot, it is his question, and he asks it from a basis, an intellectual milieu and language, that is not mine. Blanchot distinguishes between Book and book, a capital distinction for which I can find no use. Grammatical validity and logical validity are not the same, as Blanchot himself would be quick to assert

> in his etymological dictionary
> Ernst Klein gives no meaning
> to the term 'book'
>
> closest he gets
> is to connect German buch
> with buche, 'beech', saying 'The
> connection between book and beech
> is due to the Teutonic custom
> of writing runic letters on
> thin boards of beech.' This is
> as close to it as I can get